AMERICAN QUILTS

A M E R

QUI

THE STUDIO
PUBLICATIONS INC.

I C A N

L T S

BY ELIZABETH
WELLS ROBERTSON

381 FOURTH AVENUE
NEW YORK CITY

THE STUDIO PUBLICATIONS, INCORPORATED

Printed in U. S. A.

CONTENTS

The author and publisher wish to acknowledge with sincere thanks the collectors and museums who have loaned material for this book. Special acknowledgment is due to the Index of American Design in Washington for the loan of photographic material from their files.

AMERICAN QUILTS

PART ONE

BEGINNINGS

A quilt is anything made of two pieces of material with padding between and held together with stitches. But were we to end our definition on so utilitarian a note we should altogether miss the fascinating story of a craft which inherently touches upon all aspects of the life of the people of early America.

If we first take into consideration how American quilts came into being, we see them as the practical necessity they were in the earliest days. If we next consider the conditions under which they were made, we understand the struggle of the pioneer women, lightened occasionally by the gay social event of the quilting bee. Next, through the materials sewn together on the quilt tops we can visualize clothing fabrics of the women of the early days, the patterns and the weaves. Here we must also touch upon the growth of the industry which produced these fabrics from raw materials, and in so doing see the conditions of the workers and the political maneuvers of the time. And lastly, if we look at the quilts themselves, we see what design influences surrounded the quilt maker and what inspired her to the heights of the artistic expression she achieved. Thus the complete story of the American Quilt would take longer to tell than any of our great grandmothers tales at a quilting party. We can, however, outline briefly the colorful story that would comprise the background of all the early quilts that might now cover the maple and mahogany beds in our American Colonial homes in different parts of the country.

By visiting areas off the beaten track of our eastern states where people live in Colonial houses, we can still find articles made by the early settlers that are used every day. A visit to an old farm house in the lake and mountain districts of Maine, for instance, will reveal that art in the early days of America was not derivative but indigenous, growing from the hands and hearts of men and women working together to make a beautiful and comfortable place in which to live.

America had the good fortune to be settled at a time when handicrafts in England had reached a very high point of development. Although our forefathers brought over with them a great variety of furniture and other household effects, the greater number of early settlers brought only the memory of such pieces and to a greater or lesser extent a knowledge of how they were made. Many trained craftsmen brought tools, others were able only to bring an accurate mental picture of these tools, with the intention of making new ones as soon as they were needed.

The important motivating force in all early American crafts was immediate need and the quick response in ideas to meet the need. The objects made, whether they were chairs, beds or quilts, were of simple strength, fine workmanship and individual design. To understand all that is connected with the making of these objects, it is necessary to take a brief look at some of the beginnings of our cultural history. We must not forget that American quilts (despite the colorful associations they arouse in us now) were, like all other early crafts, made under tremendous strain and under almost unbelievable hardships.

In the establishment of the Colonies along the Atlantic coast, it is interesting to trace the force which made for successful colonization. The Spaniards who came first, sailed the Atlantic with the avowed purpose of finding great wealth. When these adventurers had acquired treasures enough to satisfy them most of them returned home. The influences they left behind were isolated and relatively insignificant. The French were largely *voyageurs* and they too, with the exception of the Huguenots, were impelled by love of gain and glory. The greatest lasting influence of the Huguenots, of course, is to be found in the South, with New Orleans the center of the French culture, and in the north where the results of their other colonization still exists in the province of Quebec.

The English who founded Virginia did many interesting things of more permanent value in the history of our country. Many fine estates of the wealthy planters grew from the beginnings of the London Company. The early colonization of Virginia, for business purposes, was colored by the romantic adventures of such men as Hawkins and Drake. The history of Jamestown is characteristic of the spirit of this colonization, and the restoration of Williamsburg, Virginia, gives us an idea of America under a king.

But the real cradle of America from which most of our society grew was the simple dwellings along the seacoast of New England, where men and women together had come ashore filled with strong determination to carry on their own way of life. These rugged Englishmen and women who settled at Plymouth, and the families who came later to Salem were, for the most part, as poor in worldly goods as they were firm in purpose. Not only had they left behind them most of the possessions they once owned but also a country far advanced economically, socially and culturally.

Arriving at the rocky coast of New England in the middle of December where the cold winds of the Atlantic blew over scrubby growths of oak, pines and bayberries, they landed to found a colony of their own. It is little wonder that the very first houses to be put up were merely crude shelters. Unfortunately, the first houses at Plymouth have long since disappeared but as a part of the tercentenary of Salem, which was settled ten years after Plymouth, a pioneer's village was erected which was a replica "of the windswept wilderness which was Salem in 1630." These faithful reproductions show the simplicity of the homes from which our American democracy sprang.

The first buildings put up by the settlers were sod-roofed dugouts cut into the side of a hill. Another variety of house resembled a wigwam or tent covered with the bark of trees. There was also a square, one room, shed-like building with a very steep roof covered with thatch. These were the quickest to build. Growth and development were rapid, however, and changes in the houses soon followed. Old houses all along the Atlantic coast from Boston to Portsmouth and "up beyond" in Maine show many interesting characteristics of the early colonial period. Among these were the steep roof and the overhang.

The interest in function developed through utilitarian requirements rather than from a desire for pure form. In spite of this, or perhaps because of it, fine form resulted and the products were dynamic and purposeful. Among the men who built these houses there was a strong community interest, a natural exchange of ideas, a sharing of tools and materials. At first the American house was not a castle for the individual, but rather a social and communal expression representing the best that could be constructed under the difficult circumstances.

If the lines of these houses were as straight and rigid as the principles of the people, the furniture, in like manner, was as simple as the houses. Because of immediate necessity, a sincerity of purpose was apparent in every table, chest, chair and bed made. For the making of this furniture, the nearby woods offered an abundant supply of oak, ash, walnut, maple, cedar and pine. The boards were rough-hewn and each worker planned his own design, the degree of finish depending upon the time he could afford to put into his work, and the skill of the worker.

For the most part, the very earliest furniture was as devoid of paint as the old houses. The first paint introduced was the dusty red of iron oxide and this was soon used on pine chests, tables, chairs and beds. At a much later date this was covered with a black paint which was

THE QUILTING PARTY

(*Museum of Modern Art*)

The Quilting Party. Oil painting on wood. 1840-1850. Found in Massachusetts.

(Photo: Samuel Chamberlain)

(*Photo; Samuel Chamberlain*)

Above: Samuel Slater's Mill at Pawtucket, Rhode Island.

Opposite page. Street in Slatersville, Rhode Island, named for Samuel and John Slater.

Sortwell House, Wiscasset, Maine. One of the fine houses built by a sea captain in the days when Wiscasset was a flourishing seaport and materials were brought from England and the continent of Europe to decorate the Colonial homes of America.

stencilled. As the furniture was used, the black wore off and exposed the dull red paint underneath.

As transportation increased, ships returning from England brought more and more articles that were greatly needed by the colonists. Sometimes, however, these sailing ships sank in mid-ocean, cargo and all. The wills and inventories of some of the victims give us a clear idea of the kind of furniture which was most popular then, also the value of it.

In 1646 "The Great Ship" was lost at sea, and in the wills of those who perished were listed their household goods. For instance, George Lamberton had "down and feather beds with curtains, valance and stuff for hangings." The will of another victim disposed of parlor furniture which consisted of a "bedstead and trundle bed, with curtains and bedding, a great table, a cupboard, a high and a low chair, six high stools with green and red covers." The bedroom of this householder had in it "a canopy bed with feather bedding, curtains and valance, a little cupboard with drawers, another bed, bedding, and curtains and two chests."

In studying such documents it becomes clear that, although much furniture was made in the colonies, a great deal was brought over from England. Of the various articles of furniture imported, the most expensive and the most important was the bed. The earliest beds were simple in design, built quickly for the maximum comfort with the materials at hand. The native woods were pine, fir, maple, oak, cedar and hickory. At first, posts were built in each corner with four thick boards for the frame. Holes were made in these boards and heavy ropes or cords were drawn through them, serving as a support for the mattress. These corded beds are still to be found in New England and in the backwoods of other parts of the country.

Later on, more intricate designs were introduced, based on the English and European styles imported, and soon the four-poster bed became the fashion. Under these was the trundle bed for the baby of the family. The history of the trundle bed is interesting because it goes back to the Middle Ages when the serf slept in the "truckle bed" as a protection against any intruder who might seek to molest the master who slept in the great four-poster.

These huge four-poster beds had rods under the head from which curtains were hung. The bed covering very often was made from the same material which fashioned the window curtains as well as the bed draperies. Many beds were hung with painted cotton and at a later time with toiles de Jouy from France. All this, of course, was long before material was manufactured in America with which to make these curtains, bedspreads and *quilts*.

THE EARLIEST AMERICAN QUILTS

While the men were cutting trees, squaring the timbers, subduing the wilderness by clearing, plowing and planting, the women and children were by no means idle. Between cooking the coarse food, nursing the sick, administering to the dying, they found time to daub mud on the walls of their dwellings, making the boards weatherproof. Also when the first crops came in and the first raw materials became available for home manufacture, they spun the hemp and wool and wove them into cloth. Their contribution to the cultural well-being has been much overlooked and it is a question as to whether the fore-mother was ever given enough credit for her difficult task in making the first settlements the success that they were.

It required men and women of great strength, courage, and industry to survive the terrific work and the hard winter weather. They proved that the factor necessary to a strong and enduring society was not gold nor gain, but hard work and a sense of responsibility, first to the family, then to the community.

Soon the women found that they did not have nearly enough clothes and bedding, nor sufficient quantities of materials with which to make quilts. Therefore, as clothing wore out they cut away the worn parts and saved every tiny piece that would be useful in making coverings for their beds.

From the foregoing, we can readily see how the first quilt, the *Crazy Quilt* came into being.

It was indeed crazy as far as design was concerned. There was no planned design in shape, arrangement of color or use of material. As the parent's clothes wore out, if there was a large enough area left without holes to make a child's dress or a pair of trousers for the little boy, these smaller garments were made first, then every odd shaped piece left over after that was scrupulously saved and kept together until there was enough to make a quilt.

It is interesting to note that there were two ways of making a *Crazy Quilt*. In the first, each tiny piece was fitted together like a picture puzzle and pieces were just as irregular in shape. Sometimes if the piece was too large, it was cut into smaller ones to maintain a sort of "average" in the general area of the piece. This was the beginning of organization or design. Plaid woolens were sewed next to a triangle cut from red woolen underwear. As material was woven, pieces of "lindsey," "woolsey" and "shoddy" got mixed up with all the precious all-wool materials. Linen was used and later, when chintzes and calicoes were imported from beyond the Horn, these too eventually found their way into quilts.

The second type of *Crazy Quilt* was made at a later date and in it were put scraps of silk, velvet, brocade, plush, satin, wool, cotton and linen. Bits of a wedding dress were sewed next to a piece of a scarlet uniform. These quilts for the most part were made in "blocks" (the square units of design which make a quilt). The designer determined the size of her quilt and then decided just how many blocks she wished to sew together and put into her "top."

The early quilts were large. An average old quilt was about the size of a modern sheet, 90 x 108 inches. Sometimes the blocks were large, sometimes they were small, but all had to be contained in the given area an equal number of times. When the maker of the *Crazy Quilt* of the second variety made up her mind as to the size of her block, she proceeded to baste her irregular pieces upon it. These background blocks were made of coarsely woven sacks.

The edges of the pieces in these quilts were turned in, and the seams were treated in a decorative manner—an important step from the original, unorganized quilt. A charming aspect is that the tiny bits were sewed down to the blocks with beautiful even stitches. Threads of various lengths and colors were used to make chain stitch, bead stitch, buttonhole stitch, herringbone, and all the various kinds of fagoting used in outlining. In some pieces, designs themselves were outlined. For instance, if a triangular-shaped piece suggested a fan, the ribs of a fan were outlined. Sometimes flowers and birds were embroidered on the irregular pieces, also farm and domestic animals. When the blocks were all made, they were stitched together and the top was placed over the back with a light filling in between.

In the beginning then, quilts were strictly utilitarian articles born of the immediate necessity of providing warm covers for beds. They were not laid away in chests, but were put into active use the moment they were finished. There are, therefore, few of the early quilts extant from which to make a record. But we know that within the four walls of the simple crude cabins there could have been little thought of adornment or design. Here, the mere job of physical survival was too great. We have ample evidence, however, that the inherent love of the beautiful impelled the quiltmaker to produce, as soon as she could, pieces that were decorative as well as utilitarian; and it can be said that the woman of early New England expressed herself aesthetically in her pieced quilts.

More intricate design came into the quilts when new materials could be purchased, or whenever there was enough of the old to carry through a whole quilt unit. These later developments are discussed in the chapter on "Pieced Quilts and Applique Quilts." But, before we look further into the construction and design of the different types of quilts and the fascinating names given to them, let us first take a look at the material from which they were made and also see how this was manufactured.

PART TWO

THE MANUFACTURE OF TEXTILES USED IN AMERICAN QUILTS

In examining old quilts, great admiration is immediately aroused in us for the materials used, because of the wide variety of weaves and textures. In some of the early quilts, cotton and linen were used with silk and satin. We recognize that in these fabrics such matters as spinning, weaving, dyeing and printing had become highly developed arts of long standing.

The materials in the first quilts, of course, were all imported. The bits of fabric used had been brought over by the early settlers in the form of garments, curtains and bedspreads, chiefly from England.

We know very little about the beginnings of spinning and weaving, although we have always been taught that "when Adam delved, Eve span." It is not our task here to endeavor to trace the ancient history of the craft, but rather to study the materials that were being made in France and in England at the time the pioneers were building their America and out of which they made their early quilts.

Cotton, which is the most important commodity in this research, is a plant of the hollyhock family, with a fluffy seed pod called the "boll." The best cotton we know today has a long fiber and is known as "Sea Island cotton" because it is grown on the islands off the coast of South Carolina, Georgia and Florida. It is generally considered that next to Sea Island cotton, Egyptian cotton has the greatest value. Marco Polo gave an early account of cotton as a vegetable wool growing on trees. He pictured them with sheepheads on the ends of the branches.

In England the first reference to cotton was made in 1578 when most of it was imported from Turkey, Smyrna and Cyprus, and was called cotton wool. From Calcutta, as early as 1631, The East India Company imported cotton woven into cloth called calico. This cotton cloth was soft and was referred to as linen. Indeed there was at one time a great argument as to whether it was cotton or linen and of this contention Pepys wrote in his diary on February 27, 1663, "Sir Martin Noell told us of a dispute between him as a farmer of the additional duty and the East India Company, whether calico be linen or no; which he says it is, having been ever esteemed so; they say it is made of cotton wool and grows upon trees, not like flax or hemp. But it was carried against the company though they stand out against the verdict."

In America, Columbus not only found cotton growing, but he also found cloth that had already been woven by hand. Cotton grew in abundance in Virginia but it did not become important as a commodity until after the Revolution. There were two reasons for this: The first was the discouragement by England of any cotton industry that would compete with her own, and the second was that there was no way of removing the seeds from the boll.

HOMESPUNS IN THE COLONIES

Virginia had been founded as a financial investment, or an economic experiment, which was expected to return great riches to the stockholders. This was very much the pattern of the great East India Company. The Colony was named for the Virgin Queen and great attention was lavished on it. From the first it was called the London Company, and a certain legendary glamor and romance grew around it, despite the struggling existence of the first settlers of Jamestown. However, hemp grew wild and abundantly. Flax also grew well, and it was not long before a loose homespun linen was woven. The making of this primitive linen established a regular supply of material for England. In connection with this, Lord Berkeley employed children and afterward negro slaves who were soon put to work making clothing and furnishings for the great houses on the plantations.

For a short time during the early history of the colonies, commerce was unrestricted and the settlers enjoyed free trade with England. Then the mother country imposed duties upon Colonial produce in the form of import taxes—to protect home trade. Although this was an unpopular measure, for over twenty years the first settlers, who of necessity were busily engaged in establishing their communities, still welcomed whatever textile materials came from England; but when English legislation and taxation next raised the prices of these materials, most of the colonists were forced to develop better ways of making their own fabrics, for the sake of economy. As soon as there was a room in which to set up wheels and looms, home spinning and weaving with home grown materials began in earnest. Many of these early settlers came from English households where these crafts were practiced and it was not long before native homespun was produced in quantity.

There are two interesting records—one in 1638, to the effect that spinning wheels were valued at three shillings, and the other, in 1639, (one of the earliest records in the Probate Court of Suffolk County of Massachusetts) which quotes four yards of homemade cloth at six shillings, two pence—a little over double the price of the loom. This shows the value placed upon raw materials and labor. For the most part, domestic materials were made at once into shirts, dresses, underwear, bed linen and table cloths. They were coarse and uneven in texture and neither as pleasant nor as suitable for all purposes as were the English commercial fabrics. The American weavers were discouraged until, much later, necessary improvements and refinements were brought about.

In wool, fine coverlets were woven on simple home looms and, despite technical limitations, the designs in time became very elaborate. They were first worked out on paper called "drafts" which, like quilt patterns, were passed on from one weaver to another. Itinerant weavers went from house to house to set up looms and to weave. These men were very expert and often engaged in elaborate double weaving. This type of weaving is, however, too large a subject to be dealt with here as we are really only directly concerned with the cotton fabrics out of which quilts of the period were made.

The first economic necessity of making cloth gradually changed into a social ideal and it was a great shock to England when she realized that from the elementary beginnings, weaving was becoming an important American industry—finally to help bring about economic independence. The English government had always looked upon the colonies as dependencies whose chief duty it was to supply the mother country with raw material and such other commodities that she needed. The textile manufacturers in England were surprised at the finish of the new woven materials made in the colonies and soon measures were taken to discourage its importation. The colonists reciprocated by refusing to buy English-made goods and as a result they were forced to become more and more self-sufficient in every way.

At first, the textile industry had not reached the high point of individual development as furniture making or silversmithing. While cabinet making and silversmithing were carried on in shops, weaving had remained a home craft for many years.

In 1640, however, it is recorded that William Rix, a Massachusetts weaver, built a house with the object of setting up his own loom in it. Wool, cotton and hemp were taken to him to be spun and woven into simple cloth, just as corn or wheat was taken to the grist mill to be ground into coarse flour. Other professional weavers followed suit and soon the industry began to grow so fast that the government appointed inspectors to fix prices on spinning and weaving. This was a first step in industrial regimentation. The craft product had now passed into the industrial stage.

THE EARLY AMERICAN MILLS

Cargoes of cotton and wool had been brought to the ports of Salem and Boston from the West Indies as early as 1638. In 1640 the manufacturing of wool and linen cloth was made official by the order of the General Court of Massachusetts. Included in this order was the investigation of the number of workers employed, the equipment of spinning wheels and looms, and the methods engaged in the teaching of spinning and weaving to young people. Resulting from this official order was the manufacturing by Goodman Nutt, Martin Vaderwood, John Whitney, Henry Kimball and John Witheridge, of eighty-three and a half yards of coarse linen. Crude as this material was it is the first official record of the American textile trade.

It is interesting to note that when other mills were built they were for the most part located in the upper part of stone water mills, the grain being ground on the first floor. Some of the largest textile mills in New England today trace their titles to these water rights.

So much were textiles in demand to take care of the needs of the growing population that, in 1655, Massachusetts passed a law "directing the soliciting of every town to ascertain the number of persons in each family competent to spin yarn and the fraction of their time other duties permitted them to engage in this occupation." A certain number of spinners was assessed against each household, and for every spinner it contained, a family was required to produce not less than three pounds of linen, cotton or woolen yarn a week for thirty weeks. Any family failing to produce this amount of yarn was fined twelve pence for every pound shortage.

The infant industries grew. Every colony from the topmost part of Massachusetts, now Maine, to the sunny plantations of Virginia, was actively engaged. In Rhode Island, spinning and weaving flourished during the first quarter of the eighteenth century. Other colonies such as New Hampshire, Connecticut and New York had their private and professional weavers. In Boston, a spinning school was founded in 1718, by Daniel Oliver, a merchant and "philanthropist," at the cost of six hundred pounds. The manufacture of goods soon became not a means of physical survival but a profit-making venture. Man, woman, and child became means while manufactured goods became the end or objective.

In 1753, the Massachusetts Court granted fifteen hundred pounds to buy land and build a mill. A large brick building ornamented with the symbolical figure of a woman with a distaff was erected. Like many tax-supported institutions this enterprise was abandoned, but John Brown took over the building and developed his own textile manufacturing business, advertising for sale "plain, checked and striped linens, bedticks, handkerchiefs, coating and furniture checks." Later he turned to "Bengals Lilleputians and Broglios" which indicate the influence of the extensive use of India prints at this time.

The manners and other social habits of the early colonists were very much like those of the English. Clothing indicated rank and occupation. Those who wore imported fabrics and garments were the elite. The masses wore homespun and were more "American-conscious." They had the spirit of pioneers and had yielded their allegiance to England. Calicoes were commonly used for women's dresses as they were cheap and plentiful.

THE EFFECT OF THE REVOLUTION UPON THE AMERICAN TEXTILE INDUSTRY

The English policy of making the colonies dependent upon the mother country for manufactured goods, especially textiles, helped hasten the approach of the Revolution. The Stamp Act added to the resentment regarding taxation without representation. With this new imposition added to other unfair practices, the colonies renewed their efforts to foster local manufacturers in order to lessen the dependence upon England.

Notices were posted everywhere urging the public to refrain from buying anything that was made in England and, in order to compensate for this, awards were offered to all who would contribute manufactured goods made in the colonies. For instance, the Court of Massachusetts granted fifteen hundred pounds for the encouragement of the manufacture of linen, while the New York branch of the Society for the Promotion of Arts, Agriculture and Economy offered an award for the greatest quantity—not less than five hundred yards of blue and white yard-wide linen check. England became alarmed at the turn in events. Her mills lost business and men and women, out of work, migrated to America in large numbers with their families. As they were well trained craftsmen, they were warmly welcomed in the colonies. In Boston, a committee recommended procuring a house and hiring a weaver whose wife would instruct children in spinning flax. Their board was to be furnished for three months by the selectmen of the town, and at the expiration of the three months the children were to have their own earnings. It was further recommended that the town should provide twenty spinning wheels, and a prize was offered for the first piece of linen spun and woven that was worth four shillings a yard. Spinning became popular and soon it was not only patriotic but fashionable for everyone to wear clothes made of the material they had spun and woven themselves.

This great movement toward independence grew rapidly in every field of activity. The struggle between England and the colonies became daily more acute until at last the pioneering pride and the desire for complete economic and social independence led America into war.

TEXTILES AND THE BEGINNING OF THE FACTORY SYSTEM IN ENGLAND

The political revolution in America was contemporaneous with the early stages of the industrial revolution in England. The successful application of machinery to spinning, the invention of the steam engine and other innovations were developments from which the Americans could derive no benefit, but because the machines and industrial systems were the same as those later established in America, it is important to see how this progress came about.

The textile industry owes its basic inventions to John Kay, James Hargreaves, Richard Arkwright, James Watt, Samuel Crompton and Edmond Cartwright. It is difficult to say which of these ingenious Englishmen made the greatest contribution, but the invention of the fly shuttle by John Kay in 1733 changed the whole textile industry from a hand occupation of meager output to one of power machinery. The fly shuttle was so called because of the speed with which it could be operated. By the old method the shuttle was thrown through the warp from side to side by one hand and caught by the other, thus necessitating the use of two hands.

James Hargreaves is famous for his invention of the cotton jenny. One day his little girl accidentally overturned a spinning wheel. Hargreaves noticed that it continued to revolve and the thought occurred to him that he might make a machine by which several threads could be spun at one time. On the first spinning jenny there were eight spindles—later there were as many as one hundred and twenty. The machine was named "Jenny" after his daughter.

Richard Arkwright has been called the father of the factory system because he established at Nottingham in 1769 the first practical cotton mill in the world. Horsepower was used in this mill. It was not until Arkwright's perfection of the spinning frame that warp threads of cotton could be made strong enough to meet the necessary requirements. This success with the spinning frame spurred him on to further inventions, and a new mill was built in 1771 at Cromford and run by the river Derwent. The whole operation of cotton spinning was contained here under one roof.

In 1773, Arkwright began the weaving of calicoes, having erected at Derby the first fireproof mill fitted up with the best hand looms obtainable. The power loom had not yet been invented. Because his machine could make cotton yarn of sufficient strength, Arkwright substituted this for the linen yarn previously made.

Samuel Crompton carried the idea further by spinning a thread so fine that muslin, hitherto imported from India, could be made in England. He did this by combining the spinning jenny of Hargreaves and the water frame of Arkwright. Crompton's muslin wheel, or mule, made it possible to spin yarn equal in fineness to the products of Hindu spinners.

All the inventions that improved the spinning machines increased the output of yarn to such an extent that there was a great demand for a loom that would handle the production on a large scale. The power loom invented by Edmund Cartwright resulted. The manufacturers to whom Cartwright showed his loom gave him little encouragement, and, finally, in order not to let his invention die he set up a factory of his own. Strangely enough, at first the power was supplied by a bull, but this was radically replaced in 1799 by a steam engine. Had it not been for the improvement made in the use of steam at this time by James Watt, the progress of the textile machinery in England would have been seriously handicapped. The amount of water power was limited, and the supply during the course of the year was often irregular and inadequate to meet the growing demand of industry.

By 1811, the manufacture of cloth had reached such speed and perfection in England that, so the story goes, a certain Sir John Throckmorton wagered a thousand guineas that he would at eight o'clock on a particular evening, sit down to dinner in a well-woven, well-dyed, well-made suit, the wool of which had formed the fleece on a sheep's back at five o'clock that same morning. And so it was that the wool was washed, carded, stubbed, ironed, spun and woven; the cloth itself scoured, fulled, tented, raised, steamed, dyed and dressed. The tailor was at hand to make up the finished cloth into garments, and at a quarter past six in the evening Sir John Throckmorton, winning the wager with an hour and three quarters to spare, sat down to dinner with his guests in a complete damson colored suit.

TEXTILE MACHINES IN AMERICA AND THE FIRST MILLS AFTER THE REVOLUTION

The inventions of the brilliant men who made the textile industry what it was in England, were looked at with envy by the Americans. After the Revolution, fabrics improved in weave came into the market and fine muslins replaced cotton homespun. There was no doubt in anyone's mind that Arkwright's invention had given England control of the world's textile market. At first there was nothing the Americans could do about it because the mechanical inventions were jealously guarded. Realizing the great power that was hers, England had adopted rigid measures covering the patents. Exportation of the machines or any part of them was strictly prohibited. Gradually, however, ways were found for smuggling parts of machinery out of the country. Some machines were bought in England, taken apart, boxed separately, and shipped with the label "agricultural implements"; others are said to have been cut into small pieces and shipped to France as glassware and then reshipped to America. England also tried to keep watch over her skilled workmen. There is a record of one such workman who had succeeded in boarding an American bound ship as a stowaway. Somehow this was suspected and the ship was stopped, searched, the workman seized and taken back to England.

Although the Americans had great difficulty in acquiring English textile machines, many men were at work on this side of the Atlantic trying to improve American manufacturing. One of the first of these was Samuel Wetherill, Jr., a Quaker of Philadelphia, who joined with several other Philadelphia merchants under the name of The United Company of Philadelphia.

Meanwhile, with patriotism running high after the Revolution, among the organizations that had been formed for promoting the manufacture of articles at home was the Pennsylvania Society for the Encouragement of Manufacturers of the Useful Arts, in Philadelphia.

Its prime function was to establish factories. It was pointed out to patriotic Americans that the new Republic had superior raw materials and a market at home. It also had other advantages such as exemption from duties, the ability to sell for cash, and a fine climate for bleaching the finished product.

The Board of Managers offered a prize for the most useful machine to be moved by water, fire, or otherwise. It also offered medals for the best specimen or patterns of printed linen, or cotton goods made in Pennsylvania. The advertisements for these and other prizes were seen by many textile workers in England, and, by one means or another, despite English discouragement, skilled workers arrived in America.

The first mill in New England was established at Beverly, Massachusetts, and made velvets, corduroys, dimity, fustians, denims and muslin. It was owned by John Cabot, George Cabot, Deborah Cabot and others. In 1791 George Cabot wrote to Alexander Hamilton that the number of employees was forty, thirty-nine of whom were native. In 1789, George Washington visited this mill on his Presidential tour and commented upon the excellency of the fabrics being produced.

Washington was much interested in textiles for he knew all about spinning and weaving on his own plantation at Mount Vernon. In the same year (1789) he visited The Boston Sail Cloth Factory about which he wrote: "They have twenty-eight looms and fourteen girls, spinning with both hands, the flax being fastened at the waist. Children (girls) turn the wheels for them; and with this assistance each spinner can turn out fourteen pounds of thread a day when they stick to it; but as they are paid by the piece or the work they do, there is no other restraint upon them but to come at eight o'clock in the morning and return at six in the evening. They are the daughters of decayed families—none others are admitted."

Although better textiles were being produced (as well as imported) in America after the Revolution, there was not a single Arkwright machine in this country until 1790, when Samuel Slater constructed the first one in Pawtucket, Rhode Island. He built it entirely from designs he had memorized.

SAMUEL SLATER—THE FATHER OF THE AMERICAN TEXTILE INDUSTRY

How it was that Samuel Slater, a young mechanical genius, left England and came to America is recorded in the following way. One of the Philadelphia papers came to his attention in which there was mention of an award for anyone succeeding, or partially succeeding, in constructing a carding machine. Apprenticed to a partner of Arkwright, and now superintendent of the mill, young Slater was filled with new ambition. He carefully memorized in detail the plans for the Arkwright machines and secretly made plans to emigrate.

After arriving in this country he looked around for the best opportunities available to him, with the knowledge he possessed. He found New York unsatisfactory, but came in contact with Mr. Moses Brown of the firm of Almy and Brown, of Providence. For a price, he promised Brown to construct a machine based on the principle of Arkwright's, but he made the provision that if it did not work he would make no charge for his material or his time. Brown bargained with Slater and eventually took him into the firm, making it Almy, Brown and Slater, and the mill at Pawtucket, already referred to, was started. So great was the secrecy maintained while the work of building the machinery was in progress, that all the construction was done behind closed shutters. A water frame of twenty-four spindles was made, two carding machines, and the frames necessary for the spinners. The necessary iron work was forged by Wilkinson, whose daughter later became Slater's wife. At the very first, the power was supplied by an old Negro but water power was later installed. His project was a tremendous success and Slater became the acknowledged founder of the American textile industry.

(Photo; Courtesy Samuel Chamberlain)

(Photo; Courtesy Mrs. Winchell)

Above: Field bed with simple four posts, plain fish net canopy, and applique bedspread in a house at Rockport, Massachusetts. Below: Field Bed with netted tester in the Gilman Mansion, Brunswick, Maine. The quilt is a fine old example of applique with the "Rose of Sharon" pattern.

(*Photo; Samuel Chamberlain*)

Bedroom in the Warner House, Portsmouth. The curtains and tester are of Toile de Jouy.

"L'Hommage de L'Amérique à la France." An example of Toile de Jouy printed cotton (French, 1785-1790) designed by J. B. Huet and printed at Oberkampf's factory. This pattern was used on the tester of the bed illustrated above. On the curtains of the same bed, the fabric illustrated at the top of the opposite page was used.

(*Metropolitan Museum of Art*)

"Quatre Parties du Monde." Detail from a J. B. Huet design in Toile de Jouy, made in 1781.

(*Art Institute of Chicago*)

Below: Netted tester with copperplate print bed quilt, in a bedroom at Haskell House, West Gloucester, Massachusetts.

(*Photo; Samuel Chamberlain*)

(Photo; Courtesy, Samuel Chamberlain)

Above: Four poster bed, without tester, in a bedroom at Cape Ann Historical House, Gloucester, Mass. The quilt is patchwork in "Variable Star" design. Opposite page, top: Field bed with netted canopy of airy grace in a bedroom at Whipple House, Ipswich, Massachusetts. Opposite page bottom: Field bed of unusual width, with trundle bed under it, in a guest room at Wayside Inn, South Sudbury, Massachusetts. Washington, Lafayette, Longfellow and Edison are all reputed to have slept in this room. "Wayside Inn" was built in 1686.

(*Photos; Courtesy, Samuel Chamberlain*)

(*Photos; Courtesy, Samuel Chamberlain*)

On the two canopy beds illustrated here are fine examples of the "All-white" quilt. Above: A bedroom in the Governor Beming Wentworth House, Portsmouth, New Hampshire. The wallpaper is the original which was brought from England in 1750. Below: A beautiful field bed with reeded four posts and net tester in the Governor Christopher Gore House, erected in Waltham, Massachusetts, in 1804.

Above: This bed, made by an early carpenter named Ward, from Wiscasset, Maine, shows elaborately carved posts with plain canopy boards. The applique quilt has a star pattern with alternating blocks of copperplate chintz. Below: Detail of an old quilt made by Sophia Foye in Wiscasset, Maine. The "Variable Star" pattern is in brown, lavender, and cream. The quilting is in simple lines parallel with weaver and the alternating blocks are made of copperplate cotton prints.

(Courtesy, Miss Sortwell and Mrs. Winchell)

(*Chicago Historical Society*)

Maple bed (and trundle) with pieced quilt—made in Fort Dearborn and sold to help raise money to build the First Presbyterian Church of Chicago. The quilt is made of two designs of printed gingham.

At the start, because labor was hard to find, only children were employed at the mill. These children were from eight to fourteen years old and received from $1.30 to $1.40 per week. The indoor work was hard and disciplinary measures were required, but in 1793, Slater started what was reputedly the first Sunday School in America.

Out of these beginnings, whole families were soon employed and this led to the convergence of groups of people wholly dependent upon the mill.

Slater produced so much yarn that marketing it soon became a problem. Commission houses sprang up and agents, or merchants, were employed to dispose of the yarn to individual women for the purpose of weaving fabrics (for everyday wear) upon their own looms at home. These commission houses appeared in such cities as Salem, Boston, New York, Philadelphia and Baltimore.

If all credit goes to Samuel Slater for establishing the Arkwright machine in America, thereby making it possible to produce warp from cotton instead of linen, to Mrs. Slater goes credit for the first cotton sewing thread, produced by her on her own spinning wheel. This was the start of a great new industry in itself.

The success of Slater and his American use of the Arkwright machines became famous throughout the country, and men who worked with him went out to build their own mills and establish their own fortunes. Many of these mills were successful but others failed for one reason or another. One mill was built at Warwick, Rhode Island, a second in Pawtucket, and another in Cumberland, Rhode Island. One of Slater's Pawtucket mill hands built the first cotton mill in New Hampshire. Indeed it has been said that within three years after the completion of Slater's first mill in 1791, ten mills were established in Rhode Island and one in Connecticut. By 1809 there were no less than eighty-seven mills in the Eastern States.

As these mills continued their increase in output, home weaving was no longer able to keep pace. Power looms had not yet been introduced and the inevitable overproduction of yarn occurred. Moses Brown became very much alarmed and wrote to Slater: "Thee must shut down thy gates or thee will spin all my farms into cotton yarn." Some sort of remedy had to be found but strangely enough, when plans for a power loom were later offered to Slater he refused them.

John Slater, a brother of Samuel, came to America in 1803 and brought with him new ideas and a knowledge of improvements in English machinery. He set out to find a site for a mill and decided upon a place called Smithfield, which was later called Slatersville. John joined his brother's company and in 1807, Almy, Brown and Slater began spinning at Slatersville. John Slater was less conservative than Samuel and was enthusiastic about every new invention. When William Gilmore approached him with plans and models for a power loom, John gave him great encouragement. However, Samuel was much more loath to yield to new ideas and he turned William Gilmore away. If Samuel Slater had listened to his brother, he not only would have been the first to construct a mill with spinning machines, but also with power driven looms. The whole process could then have been completed under one roof.

William Gilmore, though unsuccessful in selling his ideas to the Slaters, carried them to Judge Daniel Lyman of North Providence. By his acceptance of Gilmore's offer to build a power loom another milestone had been reached from which all mill owners benefited.

Samuel Slater not only achieved great wealth for himself and his associates but placed cotton manufacturing in the United States on a permanent basis. Next he started to make wool yarn and, at the time of the war of 1812, he was without doubt the leading manufacturer in the United States.

While the Slaters and Gilmore had made great improvements in spinning and weaving in the Eastern States, Eli Whitney in 1792, had invented the cotton gin* and the South was developing its own cotton industry.

* An invention which removed the seed from the "boll." It is said that before Whitney made this, it took a man a year to do what Whitney could do in a day.

Thomas Jefferson spoke of employing in his own household two spinning jennies, a carding machine, and a loom with a flying shuttle, by which were made more than two thousand yards of cloth a year for his family and servants. In a letter he said: "The four southermost states made a great deal of cotton. Their poor are almost entirely clothed in it in winter and summer. It is as well manufactured as the calicoes of Europe."

A visit to Mount Vernon is not complete without a study of the weaving house built for George and Martha Washington's weavers. Letters show the meticulous accounts kept by President Washington pertaining to all work. The bedrooms revealed the work and good taste of the first First Lady, for on her bedsteads were coverlets and quilts made by her servants under her direction.

The first mill in the world where the whole process of cotton manufacturing was carried on by power was that of the Boston Manufacturing Company, incorporated at Waltham in 1813 and known as the Waltham Company. This grew out of visits to the mills of Scotland and England by Francis Cabot Lowell. Here again the founders of the mills had no mechanical drawings to guide them. Lowell himself invented a power loom which in 1816 turned out cotton material a yard wide. This looked like the unbleached cotton made in India which had been imported in great quantities for a number of years. The company had great competition from England, but prospered well in spite of this. A new mill was built on a site eventually named Lowell which, as is known, has become one of the most important textile centers in the United States.

SOCIAL CONDITIONS OF THE AMERICAN FACTORY WORKER

As the textile industry grew and prospered great changes occurred simultaneously in the nation. During the Colonial period and up to about the beginning of the nineteenth century, textiles were a home craft. Then the introduction of the machine turned the rivers and waterfalls of New England into the power that manipulated spinning frames and looms. Great opportunity was offered to the inventive genius of the people. Quiet, calm New England changed from the great shipping center it had become to crowded, noisy, manufacturing communities, which developed rapidly. Money poured into the mill owners hands and still more money came. The clear blue skies of villages were clouded by the smoke of busy factories.

Inevitable social changes were brought about by the newly developed factory system. At first, in Pawtucket, Slater employed sons and daughters of his friends and neighbors. He had a fatherly, personal interest in his employees. Children were put to work. Of the first nine youngsters employed seven were boys and two were girls, ranging in age from seven to twelve years. Soon there were over one hundred children from four to ten years of age working full time at Slater's mill.

As the industry grew, more help was needed. As far as possible the Rhode Island System of employment (as Slater's system was called) was to employ whole families. These families were paid in goods supplied by the company and not in cash. As long as the mill was operating, everyone was taken care of—but when work became scarce, entire families were without supplies and great hardships resulted.

The Waltham System of employment was different to Slater's. When Francis Cabot Lowell introduced it in his mill he realized that he must have adult workers and the only adults unemployed were women. The sole exception to employed women at this time was the poorly paid school teacher. In order to attract women to his factory, Lowell opened boarding houses operated by the company. Girls from farms poured into the mills because of the economic independence offered to them. Some remained long enough to become valuable permanent operators, but many were tempted only by what seemed to them to be an opportunity to broaden their social experience or to earn enough money to buy a greatly coveted trousseau.

Many workers became discouraged and returned to the farms because as time went on conditions in the Waltham System deteriorated. Native born women mill workers were replaced by Irish and French Canadians who were willing to work for less money. They, in turn, and for similar reasons, were driven out by emigrants from Poland, Bohemia and Italy. These people were unfamiliar with American standards of living. They were satisfied to live in crowded tenements, cheap flats and small houses supplied by the mill owners.

Slums resulted as the mill cities increased in population and laws to fix responsibility and avert abuses of various kinds became necessary. Wages and hours were gradually fought for. It is not easy to imagine the frightful conditions of extreme poverty which existed for the factory workers at this time. In 1843, Dr. Josiah Curtis reported to the American Medical Association on conditions existing in Lowell and Boston. "The dwellings of the poor are mostly filthy, often from neglect on the part of the landlords, who get large rents and do not provide suitable drains, privies, yards, etc. The number of families in a house varies with the number of rooms. I have found from six to forty or more in one house of two stories, eleven and more in one room constantly, and eight in one bed." Dr. Henry Clark made a similar report concerning Boston. Among other places described was a cellar which served as a home for thirty-nine persons.

The Lowell Mills had originally been established by men who were sincerely desirous of maintaining a high standard of morals and right living among their employees; but from about 1840 onward, as the stocks of the corporations became more widely distributed, the attitude changed from an individual sense of responsibility to disinterested desire for profits. Moreover, although the foreign element had not yet entered the factories to any great extent, the fact that many girls became enamored of the low life and its freedom and others had failed to save their money and for one reason or another were unable to return home, tended to form a permanent factory population and labor supply. This gave the factory owners an advantage in dealing with strikes and increased their power over the mill hands.

As the prosperity of the mills increased, they became more and more crowded with workers, and conditions deteriorated still further. As stated in Curtis' medical reports "the air in the rooms where the girls worked, which ought to undergo an entire change hourly, remains day after day, and even month after month, with only the precarious change open doors occasionally give. There being no ventilation at night the imprisoned condition of many of the rooms in the morning is stifling and almost intolerable to unaccustomed lungs. After the day's work is ended, two hours release is enjoyed, a part of which is frequently spent in a crowded lecture-room, and then they retire to dormitories scarcely better ventilated than the mills. From four to six and sometimes eight are confined during the night in a single room of moderate dimensions."

In such mills as had now adopted the Waltham System, the mill hands were considered more as part of the mill machinery than as human beings. In 1885, the manager of the largest mill in Fall River said that so long as the hands were able to work, he would get all that he could out of them, and when they gave out and could not work any longer, he replaced them as he would worn out parts of the machines.

The Fall River petition of 1842 stated that in consequence of the influx of foreign laborers, whose habits of cheap living enabled them to work at very low prices, the wages of the workmen in many of the departments of the manufacturing establishments were reduced so low as to be wholly insufficient to enable them to obtain for themselves and their families the necessities and conveniences of life. The exodus of the American worker began at Fall River, Rhode Island, and at Lowell.

In the period of 1840-1850, the labor movement had been entirely defensive. It was an effort to provide a certain standard of living, a decent outlook on life and social well being for the man and the woman who offered themselves as workers in the new industrialism which no one as yet understood. In 1850, agitation for the ten-hour law began to get into politics and labor became an integral part of the whole humanitarian movement of the times.

PART THREE

FABRICS USED IN QUILTS, THEIR COLOR AND DECORATION

The materials woven on the early domestic looms and, later, on the power driven factory looms were used for all types of wearing apparel and household necessities. The designs of these fabrics varied. Some were plain, others were figured, such as herringbone, birds-eye and honeycomb. These were the staple fabrics and, whether bleached, dyed or printed, they were much treasured, for, after serving one or more purposes they could be used again—for quilt tops. The following are the most common types of cotton fabrics found in the American quilt.

Calico. A printed fabric of plain weave, formerly much used for dresses, commonly found with dark background and small white figures, obtained by means of discharge printing but made also with small designs printed on a white background. The name was taken from Calcutta because most of the fine printed cotton fabrics originally came from there.

Cambric. A closely woven fabric of plain weave, characterized by a soft finish and a slight gloss on one side obtained by calendering. This was named after Cambrai where it was first made.

Chambray. A smooth, soft cloth of combed yarns and plain weave, very similar to gingham but without pattern. The warp threads are of one color and the filling is white, the selvages always being white.

Chintz. A drapery, curtain fabric usually of plain weave and fine cotton yarns. It is generally printed with small, bright floral patterns. When treated on one side with a coating of wax and pressed with hot rollers it is called glazed chintz.

The forerunner of our modern chintz originated in India. The word "chintz" means, in the Hindu language, colored or variegated, and was brought to the western world in the sixteenth, seventeenth and eighteenth centuries by the Portuguese, the Dutch, and the English. The material was called "chintz," "toiles peintes," "perses," "Indiennes." The earlier examples were patterned in typical Indian floral and tree motifs by an elaborate process of wax resistant and a combination of mordant and indigo dyeing. The method was superseded by wood-block printing, copperplate printing, and roller printing.

Cretonne. A plain and figured woven material printed and used for curtains and draperies. It is generally heavier and coarser than chintz.

Gingham. A plain woven, yarn-dyed fabric, woven in stripes, plaids and checks. It was originally made in India.

Longcloth. A closely constructed, fine grade cotton cloth made of softly twisted yarns in plain weave. It is bleached and given a light sizing.

Muslin. A fine cloth of plain weave, with greater body than cambric. The name came from Moselle.

Nainsook. A soft fabric of very fine plain weave, used for babies clothes and fine lingerie.

Percale. A closely woven fabric made of good grade cotton in plain weave and printed with rather small geometric figures after bleaching. It is given a slight starch finish and is used chiefly for dresses and shirts. Combed cotton yarns, woven into high count fabric, form the high grade sheeting known by this name. This material was greatly desired by quilt makers.

Prints. Plain woven staple cotton fabrics with simple all-over printed designs are referred to as "prints."

Turkey Red. A plain unsized cotton material of a brilliant red color, practically fast, was originally colored with vegetable dyes from Turkey and frequently used in quilts.

BLEACHING FABRICS

Before the cotton fabric was made into quilts, even before it was dyed, it was necessary to bleach the material. The fabric, as it was taken from the loom, was a dull gray color which neutralized any dye and in order to obtain a brilliancy of color in the material, it was necessary first to bleach it. This dullness is due to the fact that the cotton fiber contains about five per cent of such impurities as gums, waxes, and oily substances. The resulting dull gray tone is not a serious consideration if the fabric is to be dyed black or any other deep color. But even if the cloth is to be dark, it still must be scoured sufficiently to remove the oil. This treatment consists of removing wax or fatty substances by boiling in solutions of soap, sodium carbonate, caustic soda, or mixtures of all three.

Bleaching may be done in the yarn or in the fabric. If it is to be done in the fabric, the process is much more complicated. In general, there are three processes: the white bleach (or market bleach), the turkey red bleach, and the printer's bleach, which prepares the fabric for calico printing.

Bleaching, like spinning and weaving, used to be done at home. The yarn or the woven cloth was soaked in cold water and spread out on the grass to dry in the sun. A mild acid was used at first to aid in the whitening process. Sour milk was used in some places and in others linen was soaked in buttermilk before it was laid out on the grass. The juice of lemons was used in India. As the linen lay for months on the grass, much of it was stolen and strict laws had to be introduced in order to prevent this. In 1728, a bleaching field was established in Galloway, Scotland, and a premium of two thousand pounds for the establishment of other bleacheries throughout the country was granted. The bleaching greens of Ireland were, of course, famous.

As time went on, the acid of natural substances such as sour milk and buttermilk was produced chemically. Sulphuric acid was used. This was effective as a bleach but it often had disastrous effects on the fabrics, and for a time there was law against its usage. Chlorine was the most valuable of the artificial bleaches. This was used first in 1774 in Sweden, but greater success with it, as a bleach, was achieved in France in 1785. In England, chlorine was introduced as a bleach in 1786. But it was Thomas Henry who removed from the chlorine its obnoxious odor and who evolved a saturated solution of chlorine of lime which gave better results.

THE DYE POT

The principle of dyeing can be simply stated, although the dyer himself must have a thorough knowledge of chemistry—a subject too technical to be gone into in detail here. The dyer must know of what chemical substances his textiles are composed and for what other substances these textiles have affinities. With this knowledge he must seek the combination of dye materials that will give the color desired and at the same time have the proper attraction for the textile. Wool attracts some substances, silk others, and cotton still others.

The dye is simply mixed with water and into this the textile fabric is immersed until it is thoroughly soaked. The coloring matter fastens itself upon the textile or combines with it. The transfer of the coloring matter from the dye liquor to the textile has been explained by chemists as being caused by definite affinity or attraction between the dyes and the textiles.

Dyes are usually classified as natural or artificial. Natural dyestuffs have been used from time immemorial.

Natural Dyes. A small group of natural dyes like cochineal and squid sepia, is produced from animals. Another group is taken from minerals, and we have such dyes as Prussian blue, chrome yellow and iron buff. The largest source of natural coloring materials lies in the plant world. Color can be extracted from a limitless number of barks, roots, leaves, flowers, berries, and nuts by those who understand the process. Among these natural sources of dye are: indigo, logwood, fustic, cutch, butternut, sumac, madder, brazilwood, quercitron, sunflower, peachwood, canwood, Persian berries, turmeric, mustard, saffron, henna and cudbear.

The cultivation of the indigo plant and the manufacture of the dye were very early recommended. The early quilt makers were skillful in the use of the dye pot and many of the very old quilts are still clear in color.

Artificial Dyes. Natural dyestuffs were the only ones available, so far as we know, until sixty or seventy years ago when an entirely different class of colors was discovered. These are the artificial dyes that are manufactured from coal tar, a by-product obtained in making coke. Since the discovery of these dyes by Sir William H. Perkin in 1856 chemists all over the world have experimented with new colors and shades. Up to the time of the first World War, Germany had become the leading producer of coal-tar dyes, and the countries that had depended upon her for their dyestuffs suffered much inconvenience in the early years of the war. The United States, too, was thrown upon her own resources for producing dyes, and the effect of inexperience was quickly seen. Both manufacturers and dealers refused to guarantee the fastness of any color. After the war, the dye situation in America changed, and now, of course, there are many companies making dyes which are as satisfactory as the foreign dyestuffs.

In well-dyed goods, each individual yarn is evenly colored; the face and the back are the same color. The chemical composition of the dye liquor, the strength of the color, the temperature of the water, the length of time the cloth shall be kept in the dye bath, and the succeeding treatment of the material are all problems that must be worked out by the trained chemist or dyer before any dyeing operation begins. Satisfactorily dyed materials, then, are those with a clear, even color of desired tone, which neither crack nor bleed and will remain unchanged under normal conditions and usage for a reasonable length of time. It must be noted that some materials are fast to washing but not to sunlight, while others are fast to sunlight but not to washing. The ideal, of course, is to have the fabric fast under both conditions.

While a complete understanding of the dyeing operation necessitates a knowledge of chemistry, there are a few practical principles that greatly influence successful dyeing. For instance, all material must be clean in order to take an even dye and clear, pure water should be used as the liquid. It has been said that New England was fortunate in having good water as well as other conveniences for textile manufacture: hence many bleaching and dyeing plants were founded there. While there are many processes of dyeing, we are most interested here in those which were used in the making of fabrics used in quilts.

Yarn Dyeing (or Skein Dyeing). This is a very popular and direct method of coloring. It allows the introduction of many colors in the same piece of goods and gives a limitless variety of stripes, checks, plaids, figures, borders and two-toned effects. If individual figures are desired in yarn-dyed fabrics they are usually of geometric forms, as shown by squares, triangles, stars and circles often found in shirting madras and sometimes in cretonnes.

Tie-Dyed Patterns. In India a variety of patterns were produced by the process called "tie-dye" or "tied and dyed." In tie-dyed materials certain places in the undyed cloth are picked up and string is wound so evenly and tightly around these spots that no dye can penetrate to them. The entire piece of cloth is then dipped in the color bath. If an elaborate pattern is desired, many spots are tied and the cloth is dipped several times. The production of patterns in this way is a slow process, also requiring a good knowledge of difficult color combinations.

In its earliest stages, dyeing was used only to impart a uniform color to a textile. The whole surface was made one color. The first patterns to appear on fabrics were woven in, embroidered, painted or printed on by hand. The hand painting process used first in India was long and therefore expensive to undertake. The colors were beautiful indeed and the designs consisted of floral sprays taken from such exotic blossoms as the mangrove, poppy, tulip, pomegranate, anemone, peony, and magnolia. The artist of India not only produced in lovely color the beauty of the native flowers but often depicted scenes from life, literature and religion.

HANDPAINTING AND PRINTING ON COTTON

Some of the handpainted fabrics combined the old resist dye process. This is well described in "A Brief Guide to the Oriental Painted, Dyed and Printed Textiles," published by the Victoria and Albert Museum, in London. A resist is a substance, such as wax or clay, which is applied to certain parts of a fabric before dipping it into the dye vat; the resist protects the parts covered against absorption of the dye. It is impossible to name the date or the place of the origin of resist dyeing. There are early indications that it was used in Peru, India, China, Japan and most of all in Java.The Javanese used an elaborate process of resist dyeing called "batik." The pattern is traced on both sides of the material in melted beeswax which is held in liquid form in a little vessel with a spout called the "tjanting."

"Parts of the cloth which were intended to be left white, or to receive another color were covered with wax. The cloth bearing its wax coating is steeped in a dye vat and the wax is afterward removed. The process is repeated for each color required. Sometimes the wax cracks while in the dye vat, causing little lines or veins to appear somewhat like a crackle glaze in old Chinese pottery."

Handpainting on cotton had its biggest success in India and a great vogue was created for these pieces in all parts of the world. It is believed that these gay fabrics first found their way to the Fair of Saint Germain in 1658. They were extremely popular among those who could afford them. Some ambitious French designer then conceived the idea of producing such cottons, not by the tedious method of handpainting each one separately, but by means of printing many of the same design from hand carved wooden blocks.

Wood Block Printing. This idea of wood block printing proved a success and workshops in several provinces in France began to produce cottons printed in this manner. Though lacking the characteristic charm of the Orientals, they were delightful and colorful, nevertheless, and women of ordinary means bought them for their dresses, bedroom curtains and bedspreads. These cottons, characteristically Indian in color and design, were called "Indiennes." Soon they became so popular that the manufacturers of silk, velvet, tapestry and other materials in France were forced to declare themselves bankrupt and sought the help of the government. The result was that laws were enacted which not only prohibited the importation of Indian fabrics but also closed all wood block printing workshops in France. The Edict of October 26, 1686, ordered the destruction of all blocks used in printing, and prohibited the sale of all printed cottons, whether they were Indian importations or French reproductions. It further authorized that all printed fabrics found in shops be burned and the merchants heavily fined. As a result of this, many who had worked at this craft were driven from the country—but not all. The feminine desire for lovely fabrics was not to be thwarted and as the demand became greater than ever, printing was continued in secret warehouses.

In England, the story was much the same as it had been in France. Painted Indian cottons became extremely fashionable. As early as 1831, the East Indian Company was granted permission to import satins, taffetas and painted calicoes into England. Then later, the painted Indian cottons became extremely fashionable among the elite with the result that money was poured into the East India Company instead of being earned by manufacturing companies at home. To protect the domestic manufacture of prints, an act was passed in 1700 which banned the importation of all decorated cottons from the East Indies, Persia and China.

The agitation against the use of printed cotton reached an all time high in 1722 when an act was passed prohibiting the use of all decorated cottons. This was brought about by the workers in wool and silk who had become extremely jealous and fearful that their own business might be ruined.

Much later, ambitious and enterprising manufacturers in England (and also in France) were permitted to set up print works to imitate the beautiful painted India cottons. In England, in 1770, Sir Robert Peel founded a company at Bury in Lancashire and made many prints especially for the American trade. One good example of this is the copperplate called "Penn's Treaty with the Indians." Indeed, England made some very creditable prints which paralleled in an interesting way the patterns found in the Liverpool porcelain ware of that time.

English women of the period took great pride in their calicoes both for dresses and for furniture coverings. The brilliancy of the color, the fineness of the weave, the fastness of the dye, and the beauty of the designs were all matters of great concern.

In her book "Weaves and Draperies," Helen Churchill Candee wrote that "all France and all England flowered like a June garden and the cottage interior became as gay as madame's boudoir. All honor to the venturesome little ships that sailed East and brought home a beauty which inspired the development of one of the world's greatest industries. Silk had furnished houses and dressed the persons of the rich for centuries, but homespun linen and wool had been the apparel of the cottages. It is not difficult to imagine the happiness which the gaily flowered cotton fabrics gave the women of the time for their homes and their own attire."

Toiles de Jouy. Of all the various manufacturers of printed cotton, the greatest was Christophe Phillipe Oberkampf who founded the company for printing cottons from wooden blocks at Jouy, near Versailles, France. During the period of the ban on printed cotton, Oberkampf, had traveled everywhere learning all the complicated processes of dyeing and printing. When he was able to open up his factory, he employed the finest artists and engravers that it was possible to obtain. Unfortunately, in other factories of the time, the designs were made by engravers who were not artists and, while the printing was technically good, the design was uninteresting and many times artistically bad. At Jouy, splendid taste was shown in the patterns, the dainty flowers, the attractive stripes and the whole composition of the design.

The process of block printing at the Oberkampf factory at Jouy is very interesting. First, the material was soaked in water to remove all foreign matter. Then it was mangled so that the surface was firm and smooth. It was taken from the mangle into the printing room where large blocks with the design cut in high relief were ready. The dye or ink was placed upon the blocks by means of a roller and a quick stroke of a large mallet drove the color into the fabric. Large blocks were used for curtains, wall hangings, bedspreads and furniture coverings but the greatest demand was for small designs for dress material. A different block was used for each color.

The first press for printing cotton from copperplates was constructed at Jouy in 1770. Instead of cutting the design on a wooden block, it was incised on a metal plate. This was then placed on a frame which moved under an inked roller over a wooden structure from which it fell into a basket. This was printed near a furnace so that the ink would dry quickly. With the introduction of the copperplate the technique of the designs changed. Line drawing took the place of large, free patterns of leaves and flowers. The new process was limited to a single color and as a result the toiles de Jouy were monochromatic in blue, green, brown, rose and mauve.

The next invention in printing was line engraving on metal cylinders which were mounted on a calendering frame. This roller printing machine could print over 5400 yards of cotton a day, which was the equivalent of the work of forty-two block printers. The engraving of the cylinders by hand was a long process, but in 1801 a mechanical method of achieving this by means of steel points driven into the copper was invented.

The material, once printed, was passed through the drying room, then soaked in water and put through the madder bath to fix the colors. It was soaked again then spread out on the grass of the meadows to dry. Thus, when business was good, the fields around Jouy blossomed out in brilliant colored cottons.

So popular did the toiles de Jouy become that many notable people visited the factory and among these were Napoleon and the Empress Josephine. Napoleon inspected the roller-printing machine, the presses for printing from copperplates and the department of wood block printing. Josephine was more interested in the fabrics themselves and as a souvenir of her visit, ordered some cotton prints.

One of the big discoveries in the textile world was made in Jouy in 1810, when it was found that the color green could be printed with a copperplate on a roller in a single operation. Previously green of any fastness had to be made by two successive applications—indigo blue on yellow or yellow on indigo blue. Oberkampf was awarded the grand prize given every ten years to the founder of an establishment most useful to industry and this solid green color ranked first in the report of the jury. After a second visit to the factory, this time with Empress Marie Therese, Napoleon ordered boxes of the finest "Indiennes" sent to members of the court. While speaking to Oberkampf, Napoleon is said to have remarked: "You and I wage a good war on the English, you by your industry and I by my armies. But yours is the more effective."

Many more large patterns in monotone were now designed, and among them the following well known scenes taken from fables: "Le Meunier, Son Fils et l'Ane," "Les Quatre Saisons," "La Fête Villageoise." There were many others engraved on very large copperplates by well known artists of the day, at a proportionately high price, and all achieved notoriety for Jouy. But the main work at the factory was still the "Indienne" print, for dress material, and this was what made Oberkampf's fortune.

The most gifted and the most prolific of the decorative printers of the eighteenth century was Jean Baptiste Huet who designed for Oberkampf for many years. His first pattern, designed in 1783, was the copperplate—"Les Travaux de la Manufacture," on which the artist represented, in picturesque and cleverly distributed groups, the various phases of the industry. Included are scenes of bleaching, dyeing, block printing, the preparation of the colors, the copperplate printing, the little village of Jouy with its church, the mill for calendering, the designer himself and the proprieter Oberkampf walking with his son. Even the bell used by Oberkampf for calling the employees to work appears.

Huet had two distinct styles of decorating. "Les Travaux de la Manufacture" represents the first in which detached scenes are scattered over a space with small motifs filling in the open spaces. The second was a style in which he framed his figures in scrolls of foliage combined with arabesques. Examples of this are his "Les Délices des Quatre Saisons," and "L'Hommage de l'Amérique à la France." He enjoyed depicting dogs, cats, fowls, rabbits, wolves, foxes, doves, goats, sheep, cows and horses.

There are several very interesting copperplates which depict American subject matter, such as "L'Hommage de l'Amérique à la France" in which American Indians, amusingly to us, wear ostrich plumes as head gear.

Huet took great interest in architectural style which was very fashionable in the design of this period. He framed his new designs in geometric forms, circles, ovals and other medallions. "Le Loup et l'Agneau" is an example. After the death of Huet several other artists tried to follow his style. Among these was Hippolyte Lebras. He put his figures into medallions and geometric designs. Another artist was Pinelli who designed the famous "Toiles de Scenes Romanis" and "Monuments de Paris."

Oberkampf's contribution to textiles was so great that his style has been revived time and time again. It is often said that there would have been something lacking in the eighteenth century if it were not for the printed cottons of Jouy with the brilliance and gaiety of the prints strewn with ribbons and flowers.

Other cities in France where cotton was printed were Angers, Avignon, Beautiran, Bolbec, Bordeaux, Lyons, Marseilles, Mulhouse, Munster, Nantes, Orange, Orléans, Paris and Rouen.

PRINTED COTTON IN AMERICA

After studying some of the developments in the manufacture of printed cottons in Europe which found their way into many early American quilts, we must return to our own shores to see how these were first used and what American designs developed as a result of the example set by France and England.

As many of the fabrics brought back from Europe were intended as bridal gifts, sentiment was looked for in the design. The most favored pattern was the *Tree of Life*. This expressed the eternal affection of the donor for his beloved, because in the design were to be found symbols of eternity; the bud, the flower and the fruit all growing on the same tree. Mounds of earth from which these trees, with broad trunks grew, were enlivened with all the luxuriant flora of the Orient. The bewildering designs of plants and leaves included in them exotic birds, squirrels, monkeys, butterflies and even miniature elephants.

Prosperous ship owners and sea captains also brought back rich materials for their own houses in such ports as Portsmouth, Newberryport, Wiscasset, Camden and other New England coast towns—for use as curtains and bedspreads, as well as clothing.

In America, the first printer on cotton was John Hewson. It has been said that to Benjamin Franklin goes the credit of persuading him to leave England and come to America. After establishing a calico printing works in Philadelphia, he fought in the Revolution with Federal troops, was captured by the British, imprisoned, and when he escaped he returned to Philadelphia and his print shop. His business was most successful from the first. On July 4, 1788, in a Federal Parade in Philadelphia, Hewson had a dramatic float. This was thirty feet long and thirteen feet wide. It was covered with material made in his own shop. On the float was demonstrated the various steps in the production of a piece of fine printed cotton. There was a carding machine upon which two men combed cotton; there was a spinning frame, a lace-making machine and a full sized loom upon which a workman operated a flying shuttle. At the back of the float was John Hewson himself at a table printing a colorful pattern on white muslin and Mrs. Hewson and her daughters gowned in cotton dresses printed in their own shop. Over the float waved the calico printers' flag with the motto: "May the Union Government Protect the Manufacturers of America."

The dress material printed in the Hewson shop became so popular that Martha Washington ordered dresses made from it. These designs were delightful floral sprigs and other small units which we may see today in a quilt in the Philadelphia Museum, said to be pieced by Mrs. Hewson from scraps picked up in her husband's print shop. There is a reproduction of this quilt on page 119.

Many printers worked on cotton in various textile centers in New England. The printing machine was greatly improved and cylinder printing became an important part of every American mill. Large production resulted and the prices of domestic material, originally very high, came down. The first calicoes printed from engraved cylinders were made in the works of Thorp, Siddall and Company, six miles from Philadelphia.

ENGRAVED ROLLERS FOR CALICO PRINTING

It is curious that the first man in America responsible for printing cotton from cylinders was Mathias Baldwin of locomotive fame. In 1825 with D. H. Mason he devised a way to etch cylinders of soft steel with acid. This method was used also by Thomas Hunter. Although calico now lost its place as a fine fabric, it gained in popular use and became the common material for little girls' dresses and aprons, women's gowns and men's work shirts.

PART FOUR

SOURCES OF DESIGN IN THE AMERICAN QUILT AND THE QUILT NAMES

The early American quilt was made for a very practical reason—to provide warmth. Nevertheless, during their long evenings quilt makers began putting as much design as they possibly could into their work. In the pieced quilts, designs with sharp corners and geometric forms were the most common; in applique, silhouette was usual, and because the quilts were for the most part made from tiny pieces, all-over patterns were used.

Most of these quilt makers had no training in art but they knew from ordinary life experience how to co-ordinate the activity of hand and eye. Some of the earliest quilt makers, however, had studied in the sewing schools in England and knew beautiful stitchery. Besides this, many of the colonists were well aware of the exquisite beauty of articles made for the English aristocracy. Crewel was a well-known form of stitchery on curtains, bedspreads, and chair seats. This exquisite handiwork was only for those with money enough to buy wide linen cloth and the expensive softly colored woolen yarns.

It was a far cry from the luxurious material and meticulous stitches of the embroidery of the leisurely ladies of the English court to the quilts of the hardworking American colonial women. But the urge must have been the same, regardless of means, for in the very earliest quilts, we often find very fine stitches on the crude homespun material.

The Pilgrims and the Puritans were far from a gay people, hence they chose subdued colors for their dresses. This accounts for the many pieces of brown and gray calico in the early quilts. These people were bound to a severe and simple way of life, and preferred correspondingly simple designs.

As in all folk art, the sources of design of early quilts were based on objects of use and of everyday association for which the people had great affection. They cut bits of cotton cloth into shapes of familiar objects or into shapes which somehow best expressed their thoughts and feelings of the moment. From the very fact that these early craftsmen put, so to speak, their life experiences into these designs—indeed, from the fact that they expressed what they felt rather than what they actually saw—they may be said to be the forerunners of modern design.

It is interesting to note that every woman then, and now, who loved quilts also loved her garden. This may be due to the fact that she liked to see a bouquet of color on her beds in the dead of winter, reminding her of the flowers which she cultivated so carefully during the summer—in the garden, or in her door yard.

Nature, always the greatest source of design, provided most of the basic forms that were used—trees, leaves, and vines, also birds, animals, moths, flowers and butterflies. Other nature forms which appeared in quilt designs were stars and the sun. The elements, too, were introduced by individual representations of the wind, snow, and clouds.

The lives and customs of the early settlers themselves were sources of design. Religion, for instance, was a very strong force and biblical references are found in many quilt names. The Colonial women were devout students of the Bible. Also because it affected them directly, they were well aware of what was going on in politics. If the women of today learn their politics in club meetings and at bridge parties, the Colonial women can be said literally to have sewn their politics into their quilts. Party loyalty was as strong among the women as it was among the men.

Proper names are to be found in many of the quilts. These were names of the women or girls who made the quilts or the names of the friends to whom they were to be given. Fun appeared as inspiration for designs, and games and puzzles found their way into patterns. Occupations, also tools connected with occupations and trades appeared as names.

A classification of quilt designs originating from a variety of sources is given under the respective group heads or names:

ALPHABET

Boxed I's
Double X
Flying X
Four E
Four X
Letter H
Letter X
Madam X
T Blocks
Turnabout T
X quisite

BASKETS

Basket of Daisies
Basket of Lilies
Basket of Oranges
Bread Basket
Cactus Basket
Cherry Basket
Colonial Basket
Decorated Basket
Dutch Tulip Basket
Flower Basket
Four Little Baskets
Fruit Baskets
Garden Basket
Grandmother's Basket
Grape Basket
Pierced Flower Basket
Rose Basket
Tiny Basket
Tulip Basket

BIRDS

Bird of Paradise
Birds-in-the-Air
Bird's Nest
Bluebird
Brown Goose
Buzzard's Roost
Chimney Swallows
Dove of Peace
Dove-in-the-Window
Duck Puddle
Duck and Ducklings
Duck's Foot-in-the-Mud
Flying Swallows
Four Little Birds
Fox and Geese
Goose-in-the-Pond
Goose-in-the-Window
Goose Tracks
Gray Goose
Hen and Chickens
Hovering Hawks
King's Crows
Peacocks
Peacocks and Flowers
Square and Swallow
Swallow
Swallow's Flight
Swallows-in-the-Window
Turkey Tracks
Wild Goose Chase

BUSHES AND SHRUBS

Cactus
Cactus Basket
Mountain Laurel
Sage Bud
Snowball

FLOWERS

Aster
Bells in Bloom
Black-Eyed-Susan
Bleeding Hearts
Bluebells
Bouncing Betsy
Bounding Betty
Bouquet
Bowl of Flowers
Canada Lily
Cockscomb
Crocus Wreath
Dahlias
Dahlia Wreath
Daisy
Daisy Chain
Daisy, Lazy
Daisy, Meadow
Daisy, Mission
Daisy, Wind Blown
Dogwood Blooms
Dusty Miller
Forget-Me-Nots
Garden Quilt
Garden Maze
Garden, Grandmothers
Garden, Old Fashioned
  Flower Garden
Garden Wreath
Golden Poppies
Hollyhock Wreath
Iris
Jack-in-the-Pulpit
Jonquils
Lilies
Lily, Canada
Lily, Easter
Lily of the Field
Lily of the Valley
Lily, Meadow
Lily, Mountain
Lily, North Carolina
Lily, Persian Palm
Lily, Prairie
Lily, Tiger
Lily, Water
Lily, Wood
Lotus Buds
Lotus Flowers
Mountain Pink
Narcissus
Nosegay
Nosegay, Old Fashioned
Painted Snowball
Pansies and Butterflies
Pansy Block
Peony
Peony, Double

Peony, Kentuckey
Peony, Red
Piny
Poinsettias
Poppy
Poppies, Golden
Prairie Flower
Prairie Queen
Ragged Robin
Rose
Rose, American Beauty
Rose, Applique
Rose Bud
Rosebud and Leaves
Rose, Cactus
Rose, California
Rose, Cherokee
Rose, Climbing
Rose, Complex
Rose, Confederate
Rose, Conventional
Rose, Democrat
Rose, Desert
Rose Dream
Rose, English
Rose, Foundation
Rose, Harrison
Rose, Harvest
Rose, Indiana
Rose, Irish
Rose, Love
Rose, Louisiana
Rose, Mexican
Rose, New Jersey
Rose, Ohio
Rose, Pennsylvania
Rose, Radical
Rose, Garden
Rose of Dixie
Rose of 1840
Rose of St. Louis
Rose of Sharon
Rose of Tennessee
Rose of the Carolinas
Rose Spring
Rose Tree
Rose, Texas
Rose, Topeka
Rose, Virginia
Rose, Whig
Rose, White
Rose, Wild
Rose, Wind Blown
Scotch Thistle
Spice Pink
Sunflowers
Sunflower, California
Sunflower, Kansas
Sunflowers, Three Flowered
Sunflowers, Triple
Sweet Pea Wreath
Triangular Flower
Tulip
Tulip Blocks
Tulip Bud
Tulip, Cleveland
Tulip, Double
Tulip, Dutch
Tulip, Full Blown
Tulip, Garden
Tulip in Vase
Tulip Lady Fingers
Tulips, Pot of
Tulip, Rare Old
Tulip, Texas
Tulip Tree
Tulip Wreath

FRUITS

Apple Hexagon
Applique Pineapple
Baltimore Pear
Basket of Oranges
Cherries
Cherry Blanket
Cherry Tree and Birds
Colonial Pineapple
Forbidden Fruit
Grapes and Vines
Indian Plums
Love Apple
Melon Patch
Olive Branch
Orange Peel
Pieced Pineapple
Pineapple
Pomegranite
Prickly Pear
Strawberry
Tufted Cherry

GAMES AND PUZZLES

A Boston Puzzle
Bachelor's Puzzle
Columbian Puzzle
Devil's Puzzle
Dutchman's Puzzle
Eight Hand's Round
Farmer's Puzzle
Ferris Wheel
Fool's Puzzle
Follow the Leader
Hands all Around
Jack-in-the-Box
Johnny-Around-The-Corner
Kite
Kitty Corner
Leap Frog
Lend and Borrow
Merry-Go-Round
Merry Kite
Old Maid's Puzzle
Pin Wheel
Pullman Puzzle
Puss-In-The-Corner
Reel
Right and Left
Seek-No-Further
Shoo Fly
Star Puzzle
Steeple Chase
Swing-In-The-Corner
Swing-In-The-Center
Tic—Tac—Toe
Tile Puzzle
Washington Puzzle
Whirligig

GEOMETRIC

Beggar's Block
Box Quilt
Chained Five Patch
Chained Star
Cube Work
Diamond Cube
Diamond Design
Double Pyramid
Four Patch
Fundamental Nine—Patch
Hexagonal Star
Honeycomb

Honeycomb Patch
Honeymoon Cottage
Mosaic
Nine Patch
Octagon
Octagon File
Octagon Tile
Octagonal Star
Roman Square
Square and a Half
Square and Circle
Squares and Stripes
Square and Triangle
Stripe Squares
Three Patch
Tousand Pyramids
Triangular Flowers
Triangles
Winged Square

INSECTS

Brown-Tailed Moth
Butterfly
Fly Foot
Honey Bee
Pansies and Butterflies
Shoo Fly
Spider's Den
Spider's Web
Swarm of Bees

LEAVES

Acorn and Oak Leaf
Autumn Tints
Bay Leaf
California Oak Leaf
Hickory Leaf
Maple Leaf
Oak Leaf
Oak Leaf and Tulip
Sweet Gum Leaf
Tea Leaf
Tobacco Leaf

MISCELLANEOUS

Air Castle
All Tangled Up
American Bride's Quilt (1850)
American Log Patch
Around the World
Arrowheads
Baby Blocks
Black Beauty
Blindman's Fancy
Block Album
Bow Knot
Bows and Arrows
Box Blocks
Brick Pile
Brick Wall
Brickwork Quilt
Bridal Stairway
Children's Delight
Castle Wall
Chinese Lanterns
Cincinnati Cog-wheel
Continental
Country Farm
Crazy Patch
Crazy Quilt
Crib Quilt (all white)
Cross Roads
Cube Lattice
Cupids Arrowpoint
Devil's Claws
Domino
Domino and Square
Double Hearts
Double Hour Glass
Double Monkey Wrench
Double Nine Patch
Double Square
Double Wedding Ring
Diagonal Log Chain
Dresden Plate
Drunkard's Patchwork
Drunkard's Path
Economy Patch
Eight of Hearts
Eight Point Design
Eight Point Star
Enigma
Eternal Triangle
Everybody's Favorite
Fan
Fan and Rainbow
Fan Patch
Fantastic Patch
Feather Crowns
Fence Row
Five Stripes
Flutter Wheel
Flying Dutchman
Fool's Square
Forest Path
Four Little Fans
Four Patch
Four Points
Fragrance
Framed Medallion
Friendship Knot
Gentleman's Fancy
Gift of Love
Girl's Joy
The Globe
Grandma's Fan
Grandmother's Dream
Grandmother's Fan
Grandmother's Favorite
Grandmother's Own
Greek Square
Hair Pin Catcher
The Hand
Hearts Seal
Hero's Crown
Hit and Miss
Home Treasure
Hour Glass
House that Jack Built
Ice Cream Bowl
Indian Candles
Indian Canoes
Indian Hatchet
Indian Trail
Interlaced Block
Ladies Delight
Ladies' Wreath
Lady of the Lake
Linked Diamonds
The Little Red House
Little Red School House
Log Cabin
London Roads
Love Ring
Lover's Links
Lover's Knot
Magic Circle
Maltese Cross
Maltese Crown
Memory Block
Memory Circle

Mystic Maze
Mother's Dream
Necktie
No Name Quilt
None Such
Oddfellow's Cross
Odd Patchwork
Odd Pattern
Odds and Ends
Odd Star
Old Homestead
Old King Cole's Crown
Old Maid's Ramble
Old Scrap Patchwork
Old Town Pump
Patience
Patience Corners
Paving Blocks
Pincushion
Pincushion and Burr
Princess Feather
Prosperity Block
Rail Fence
Railroad Crossing
Rambling Road
Ribbon Squares
Roman Stripe
The Royal
St. Valentine's Patch
Sawtooth Patchwork
Scissor's Chain
Shelf Chain
Ship of Dreams
Silver and Gold
Single Irish Chain
Single Wedding Ring (Wheel)
Sister's Choice
Skyrocket
Spinning Triangles
Split Nine Patch
Spools
Square Log Chain
Stepping Stones
Stone Wall
Strangers
Stuffed Quilt (all white)
Sugar Bowl
Sugar Loaf
Swastika
Swinging Corners
Tail of a Kite
Tangled Garter
Triple Irish Chain
True Lovers' Buggy Wheel
True Lover's Knot
Tumbler
The Urn
Wagon Tracks
Wondering Foot
Weather Vane
Widow's Troubles
Wheel
Wheel of Chance
Wheel of Fortune
Wheel of Mystery
Winding Walk
Young Man's Fancy
Zig-Zag

NATURE—ANIMALS

Bear's Paw
Bear's Foot
Cats and Mice
Cat Track
Elephant
Flying Bats
Four Frogs Quilt
Fox and Geese
Snail's Trail
Toad-in-the-Puddle

PLANTS

Good Luck Clover
Gourd Vine
Shamrock
Tassel Plant

POLITICS AND PLACE NAMES

Alabama Beauty
Arkansas Traveler Star
Boston Puzzle
Buckeye Beauty
California Rose
California Sunflower
Canada Lily
Chicago Star
Clay's Choice
Confederate Rose
Cowboy's Star
Cleveland Tulips
Courthouse Square
Democratic Country
Democrat Rose
Desert Rose
Fifty—Four—Forty—or—Fight
Freedom Quilt
Free Trade Block
Free Trade Patch
Garfield's Monument
Georgetown Circle
Harrison Rose
Illinois Rose
Indiana Puzzle
Indiana Rose
Indiana Wreath
Iowa Star
Jackson Star
Kansas Star
Kansan Star
Kansas Dugout
Kansas Sunflower
Kansas Troubles
Kentucky Crossroads
Kentucky Peony
Leavenworth Nine Patch
Leavenworth Star
Lincoln's Platform
The Little Giant (in honor of Stephen A. Douglas)
Lone Star
Louisiana Rose
Mexican Rose
Missouri Daisy
Missouri Star
Mohawk Trail
Nelson's Victory
New Jersey Rose
New York Beauty (1776)
Northumberland Star
Ohio Beauty
Ohio Rose
Oklahoma Boomer
Old Star
Old Colony Star
Old Tippecanoe
Ozark Diamond
Ozark Star
Peary's Expedition
Pennsylvania Rose

Philadelphia Pavement
President's Quilt
Road to California
Road to Oklahoma
Rocky Road to California
Rocky Road to Kansas
State House Steps
Rose of Dixie
Rose of St. Louis
Rose of Tennessee
Rose of the Carolinas
Savannah Beautiful Star
St. Louis Star
Star of North Carolinas
Star Spangled Banner
State of Ohio
Tennessee Circle
Tennessee Star
Texas Rose
Texas Star
Texas Tears
Texas Tulip
Texas Treasure
Tippecanoe and Tyler Too
Topeka Rose
Rail of Covered Wagon
Underground Railroad
Union
Union Star
Union Calico Quilt
Virginia Rose
Virginia Star
Whig Rose
Whig's Defeat
White House Steps
Yankee Charm
Yankee Pride
Yankee Puzzle

PROPER NAMES

Aunt Dinah's Delight
Aunt Eliza's Star
Aunt Martha's Wild Rose
Aunt Sukey's Choice
Aunt Sukey's Patch
Barbara Frietchie Star
Ben Hur's Chariot Wheel
Caroline's Fan
Cleopatra's Puzzle
Crazy Ann
Dolly Madison Star
Electa Amelia Hall and
  Her Twin Sister
Fanny's Fan
Fanny's Favorite
Flo's Fan
Handy Andy
Hobson's Kiss
Jacob's Ladder
Jack's House
Job's Tears
Joseph's Necktie
Joseph's Coat
Lindy's Plane
Lucinda's Star
Martha's Vineyard
Martha Washington Star
Martha Washington's
  Wreath
Mary's Garden
Milly's Favorite
Mollie's Choice
Mrs. Cleveland's Choice
Mrs. Harris' Colonial Rose
Mrs. Keller's Nine Patch
Mrs. Morgan's Choice
Patty's Star
Peeny Pen's Cottage
Pierrot's Pom-Pom

RELIGION

Adam and Eve
Cathedral Window
Children of Israel
Church Steps
Circuit Rider
Coronation
Cross and Crown
Crosses and Losses
Cross upon Cross
Cross within a Cross
Crowned Cross
Crown of Thorns
David and Goliath
Delectable Mountains
"Ecclesiastical"
Forbidden Fruit
Garden of Eden
Golden Gates
Golgotha
Greek Cross
Heavenly Steps
Hosanna
Jacob's Ladder
Job's Tears
Joseph's Coat
King David's Crown
Many Mansions
Path of Thorns
Pilgrim's Pride
Pilgrim's Progress
Providence
Robbing Peter to Pay Paul
Roman Cross
Royal Cross
Scripture Quilt
Solomon's Crown
Solomon's Temple
Star and Cross
Star of Bethlehem
Star of the East
Starry Crown
Step to the Altar
Tree of Paradise
Tree of Temptation
Weeping Willow and
  Dove of Peace
World Without End

SEEDS

Corn and Beans
Golden Corn

SHELLS AND FISH

Clam Shell
Fish Block
Goldfish

SOCIAL

Album Patch
Autograph Patch
The Quartette

STARS
Arabian Star
Arkansas Traveler Star
Beautiful Star
Big Dipper
Blazing Star
Braced Star
Brunswick Star
Calico Star
California Star
Chicago Star
Chinese Star
Christmas Star
Cluster of Stars
Columbia Star
Combination Star
Cowboy's Star
Crazy Quilt Star
Dew Star
Diamond Star
Dolly Madison Star
Double Feathered Star
Double Star
Evening Star
Fairy Star
Falling Star
Feathered Star
Five Point Star
Florida Star
Flower Star
Flying Star
Four Stars Patch
Free Trade Star
French Star
Geometric Star
German Star
Hunter's Star
Iowa Star
Jackson Star
Joining Star
Kansas Star
King's Star
Ladies Beautiful Star
Le Moyne Star
Log Cabin Star
Lone Star
Leavenworth Star
Mexican Star
Missouri Star
Morning Star
Mother's Fancy Star
Northumberland Star
Novel Star
Old Colony Star
Ornate Star
Ozark Star
Pieced Eight Point Star
Pierce Star
Pin-wheel Star
Polaris Star
Pontiac Star
Prairie Star
Premium Star
Rainbow Star
Ring Around the Star
Rising Star
Rolling Star
Royal Star
Savannah Beautiful Star
St. Louis Star
Seven Stars
Shooting Star
Six Pointed Star
Slashed Star
Star and Chains
Star and Crescent
Star and Crowns
Star and Cross
Star and Cubes
Star and Planets
Star and Plume
Star and Puzzle
Star and Squares
Star Lanes
Star of Hope
Star of Le Moyne
Star of Many Points
Star of North Carolina
Star of the East
Star of the Sea
Star of the West
Star Puzzle
Star and Squares
Star Spangled Banner
Star Upon Star
Starry Crown
Starry Lane
Tiny Star
Travel Star
Twinkling Star
Union Star
Variable Star
Virginia Star
Windblown Star
Windmill Star

STONES

Rolling Stone
Rocky Glen

SUN

Blazing Sun
Harvest Sun
Rising Sun
Sunbeam
Sunbeam Block
Sunburst
Sunshine

THE ELEMENTS

Flying Clouds
Four Winds
Harvest Waves
North Wind
Rainbow
Snowflake
Snow Crystals
Storm at Sea

TREES

Charter Oak
Cherry Tree and Birds
Christmas Tree
Cypress Tree
Falling Timber
Forest Pattern
Hickory Tree
Inverted Palm
Little Beach Tree
Line Oak Tree
Pine Tree
Pride of the Forest
Temperance Tree
Tree Everlasting
Tree of Life
Tulip Tree

VINES

Gourd Vine
Ivy
The Vine
Vine of Friendship

WREATHS

Crocus Wreath
Dahlia Wreath
Golden Wreath
Hollyhock Wreath
Indiana Wreath
Iowa Rose Wreath
Ladies' Wreath
Sweet Pea Wreath
Tulip Wreath
President's Wreath
Wreath of Roses
Wreath of Rosebuds

As time went on and new friends were made, materials and patterns were exchanged and old designs were given new names. This is especially true of the many star patterns. Ruth Finley points out that one quilt which she called *Indian Trail* was also called *Forest Path, Winding Walk, Rambling Road, Climbing Rose, Old Maid's Ramble, Storm at Sea, Flying Dutchman, North Wind, Weather Vane, Tangled Tares, Prickly Pear* and *Just Puzzle*. The *North Carolina Lily* was one of the quilt names which changed frequently. When people moved West, new names appeared in the quilts such as *Kansas Troubles, Road to California, Rocky Road to Kansas, Star of the West, Texas, Texas Rose, Texas Treasure* and *Ohio Rose*.

DERIVATIVE DESIGNS

Quilts shared in the great interest of the American people in all crafts—an interest which developed steadily and consistently for many years after the revolution. Inspiration for design was the same in nearly all of the crafts and often one craft would provide design for another. Indeed, the craftsmen themselves were so adept that they worked in more than one medium. For instance, Paul Revere not only made fine silver but very good engravings. The furniture painters of Pennsylvania made "fractur" drawings and water color paintings, carriage makers and chair makers carved figureheads for ships as well as exquisite fireplace frames and moldings for rooms. Iron workers and village blacksmiths made well designed weather vanes and stove backs. Sign and coach painters also painted chairs, chests and other furniture. Housewives papered and painted the walls of rooms, stencilled beds, made rugs and quilts. All of this is surely indicative of the fact that early in its history America had its own folk art.

Strong national influences appeared in early American crafts. The Pennsylvania Dutch (or Pennsylvania German) represented one of the most vital forces in regional art. Their chests, made of white oak, yellow pine and tulip wood were painted dusty red and many had a wealth of ornamentation, especially on the front panels. The German love for sentiment is reflected in the hearts, entwined initials and scrolls that often appeared. The beauty of these painted designs is recognized by present day designers as it was then by quilt makers and other craftsmen who derived inspiration from them. It was not a difficult task for any woman to redraw the tulip from one of the dower chests, reorganize the design and place it in blocks on her quilt top.

Stencilled walls, floors and furniture offered source material of a geometric nature. The designs for the stencil were especially suited to quilts because of the simplification demanded of the stencil technique.

The earliest recorded example of a stencilled wall was believed to have been made in 1778. These designs, no doubt, were in turn suggested by borders and panels of the elaborate and expensive wallpaper brought over from France and England. The background for the stencils was usually pale pink, pale blue, pale ochre or light gray. Trailing vines formed borders. Here again the bellflower, used on quilts and on pressed glass appeared. Borders of climbing roses, with laurel leaves were often used. Swags with bells or tassels were favorite motifs for friezes. Stencilled in all-over patterns were leaves and flowers, pine trees, festoons and geometric forms. Birds, plants, and animals were placed in all sorts of arrangements. Urns and simplified baskets were used. Rosettes, discs, hearts, pineapples, stars, diamonds, all supplied interesting units to wall decorations and all gave the quilt maker ideas for patterns.

Heraldic designs were sometimes used on walls in ornate frescos painted about 1796-1803. The main difference between these fresco paintings and stencilling lay in the fact that frescos were done freehand, while the stencil limited the artist to simple, flat designs. Painted and stencilled designs on such small objects as tin tea caddies and trays might also have been inspirational material, easy to adapt to quilt blocks and borders.

Another design source for the quilt maker was the stove back. Many fine designs were molded and cast in iron. The units were mostly rosettes with simply modeled vine borders,

The tailor's stove shows a low relief in the front panel which might easily have been adapted for a quilt design.

Another extremely important source of design dear to the hearts of all women is to be found in the decoration of her precious dishes. Many fine pieces of China with floral, bird and animal patterns made their way to the new country, including Royal Worcester, Royal Doulton, Copeland, Spode, Lowestoft, Wedgwood and many others. These were carefully laid away for very special use. Everyday dishes were the old blue Staffordshire ware with scenes in the centers of the plates and platters and decorative borders on the edges. At first the scenes were of England, but the astute potters soon realized that American buyers much preferred American scenes. Hence to flatter their customers they put on their dishes such prints as "The Beauties of America," or "Picturesque View of the Hudson River." Some potters sent artists to make faithful reproductions in ink or in oil of their impressions of the scenery of the new country. They also made portraits of such national heroes as Washington, Franklin, and Lafayette, and they even pictured battles of the War of 1812.

Historical scenes were placed in the center of the plates or platters, and around them were garlands of roses, lilies and other flowers. Birds, butterflies and animals also found their way into these borders. Each potter had his own arrangement.

After the eagle became the national emblem it appeared as a design in many different ways. It was carved into ships' figureheads; it was scratched onto powder horns, and among many things it was used in applique on quilts. Also in the borders of many of the plates, or as a detail of the design, the eagle often appears. The thirteen stars of the original states were used. The seal of the New Republic, with the baldheaded eagle with an olive branch in one talon and arrows in the other and with a scroll inscribed E PLURIBUS UNUM, decorated many pieces of Staffordshire. Other favorite subjects of pottery for the American market were mottoes, morals, proverbs, and maxims of Franklin.

The illustration, page 149, is a reproduction of the Lovejoy plate bearing upon it the Bill of Rights. In the medallions appear quotations, also the words: "The Tyrants Foe, the Peoples Friend." In the border are inscriptions alternating with eagles and shields; the eagles are defiant, their claws holding a sheaf of arrows and sprays of olive leaves. Scroll designs and arabesques unify the design.

The Star of the West was a plate design as well as a traditional design for quilts. *The Columbia Star* was another star pattern which appeared on the blue and white ware and which, in varying forms, was applied to quilt blocks. *The Log Cabin* belonged to the "Tippecanoe and Tyler Too" campaign and was the name given by the potter J. Ridgeway to one of the series of "The Beauties of America," which also contributed to the source of quilt design of that period.

John Clews, a prolific designer of dishes, issued three very popular sets which are highly prized by lovers of old china. They are the Don Quixote series, the Sir David Wilkie series, and the Dr. Syntax series. The latter should be mentioned especially in connection with quilts because prints of the adventures of the roving doctor were also made upon cotton in the Peel works in Lancashire, and were exported to America in large quantities, where they proved as popular as in England, for window curtains, bed curtains, valances, and bedspreads. These Syntax prints parallel closely the design found on blue dishes that were decorated by the decalcomania process.

The potters in America also used many interesting motifs which were borrowed for quilt tops. In Pennsylvania tulip ware, the pine tree was an often recurring design, also urns of flowers, natural leaf patterns, fishes, hearts and stars. A typical sgraffito pie plate, dated 1773, shows a bird, a heart, and a tulip in the decoration, together with a sentimental verse carefully lettered: "This dish and heart shall never part."

Early American pressed glass, produced before the Civil War, can be placed in much the same category of design as the china and pottery. Among these designs we find "Ashburton," "Diamond Thumbprint," "Argus," "Pressed Block," all suggesting mosaic patterns for pieced quilts. Then there were familiar patterns like *The Vine*, *Bellflower*, *Ivy*, *Inverted Palm*, *Tulip*, *Baltimore Pear*, *Cherry*, *Rose in Snow*, *Princess Feather*, *Bleeding Heart*, *Wildflower* (among others), many of which were also the names given to quilts of the same design.

The hooked rug, besides being a design source, parallels the history of quilt making in early America. Hooked or "drawn-in" or "pulled-in" rugs as they were variously called in different parts of New England, differ greatly in design. They were made in those moments between the waning daylight and darkness when the busy housekeeper had a chance to sit down—and again after supper, till bedtime. Love of home and the desire to have beautiful things at a time when materials were scarce was the first impulse of the hooker. Also, there was the same innate human urge to express oneself in material which is a common factor in all folk art. Finally, of course, it was important to many to "keep up with the Joneses" and, in such cases, this would be the necessary motivation to get them started.

Nature offered design ideas to the rug hooker just as it did to workers in other crafts. The nature of the material, however, offered opportunities for larger patterns. Rug hookers living near the seashore designed boats, lighthouses, compasses, anchors, capstans, wheels, fishes, and shells for their rugs, while farmhouses, huts, red schoolhouses, churches, bridges, picket fences, yards, gardens and villages were motifs for others. Fireplaces, interiors and clocks were also arranged in patterns.

Although pets appear in quilt designs the rug hookers featured large animals like horses, lions, tigers and deer. Also, there were geometric designs in rugs which might have suggested the mosaic patterns to the quilt maker. The diamonds, squares, ovals, scrolls and tiles appear both in rugs and quilts. In fact, the range of design in both are almost identical and in making a hooked rug, as in designing a quilt or painting a picture, there is the same element of personal preference.

In her foreword to "Early American Hooked Rugs," Alice Van Leer Carrick says: "That's why I hate what the old country women call 'boughten patches.' These completely lack the naive spontaneity which women, working by the fireside on snowbound afternoons, or in the long hours of winter evenings, were able to create upon their canvases, strips of stretched burlap, with their colors, home dyed pieces of wool and skeins of yarn. They reflected the life around them, the cat sleeping on the hearth, their memories of gold and crimson autumn, the blue of faïence upon the tall mantel." Miss Carrick also says: "Nowhere else (save in the pages of medieval miniaturists who worked with precisely the same feeling) do flowers bloom in the same profusion of unpremeditated art."

Finally, there were all other forms of needlework to inspire the quilt maker. Because Massachusetts was the center of maritime trade, frequent sailings from England to the port of Boston no doubt encouraged the sending of patterns to friends and relatives living in the New England settlements. Such designs descended from Anglo-Saxon embroideries and linens with crewel work which were used for hangings during the reign of Queen Anne. The *Tree of Life* and other designs from the far East were used. Chinese designs appeared and still other suggestions came from the Dutch East Indies. Many designs were a mixture, combined by the embroiderer in her own patterns. The stitches used were the usual Jacobean crewel work which was similar to the crewel embroidery done at Court. One very famous example of American crewel embroidery is the Mary Breed bedspread, which is in the Metropolitan Museum of Art. It was made of homespun linen in Boston in the year 1770. It is signed in the center, above a graceful floral design. Several units appear, each of which in itself is a work of art. Details from this bedspread appear on page 144.

One of the most beautiful needlepoint rugs is also to be found in the Metropolitan Museum of Art. It was made in Castleton, Vermont in 1835 by Zeruah Higley Guernsey. There are seventy eight blocks in the rug, each with a different design. The rug holds together as a unit because the background of each square is black, although the black is faded a rusty brown in some squares and greenish black in others. The green color used in the rug varies and looks as if it had been obtained by dipping the cloth into yellow and then into blue. Another unifying element in this fascinating rug is the constant use of rose and white. In some squares this rose becomes a brilliant red and in every unit white has been used as an outline or a highlight. Any one of the units in this rug would make a fine block for a quilt and the strawberry design would be particularly lovely. Any of the flower designs could easily be used in applique. The quilt is signed Z.H.G. but in one square are the letters L.F.M. and in another F.B. It is said that the two squares with these latter initials were made by two young Indians who attended the Medicine school in Castleton and lived at the Guernsey home.

MAGAZINES A DESIGN SOURCE

The illustrations in some of the early American magazines were also a design influence.

The first magazine that openly catered to women was the "A Gentlemen and Ladies' Town and Country" which was published with the avowed purpose 'to please rather than to wound, woman the noblest work of God.' The policy of this magazine was decidedly to pamper the ladies.

The second magazine to recognize the ladies was "The Lady's Magazine and Repository of Entertaining Knowledge." The first edition of this magazine states: "If the present work meets with the encouragement we expect, it is intended to adorn the succeeding volumes with an engraving to each number, with the addition of the newest and most fashionable patterns of needlework for gowns, aprons, etc. A book of this kind will be universally recommended in all boarding schools throughout the country, as it is to contain everything requisite to disseminate the knowledge of real life, portray virtue in the most amiable point of view, inspire the Female Mind with a love of religion, of patience, prudence, and fortitude. In short, whatever tends to form the Accomplished Woman, the Complete Economist, and the greatest of all treasures, A Good Wife."

In 1828, Sarah Josepha Hale started the "Ladies Magazine" in Boston and to her is given the distinction of being the first woman editor of America. She left Boston and went to New York to become the editor of "Godey's Lady's Book." She made this a truly American publication. Patterns appeared in "Godey's Lady's Book," Frank Leslie's "Lady's Gazette," "Peterson's Magazine," later in "Harper's Bazaar" and still later in "The Ladies' Home Journal" and the "Woman's Home Companion." These patterns included designs for quilt blocks and also for the quilted background. Designs appeared for braiding which could be modified for quilting patterns. The tissue paper pattern came later and various means of transferring the pattern from the paper to the cloth were devised.

PART FIVE

PIECED QUILTS AND APPLIQUE QUILTS

The earliest quilts are the pieced ones. These were not designed with any decorative effect in mind but were pieced together in order to get much needed warmth in a hurry. The origin of the first quilt, the *Crazy Quilt* we have already studied in the first chapter.

After this came the *Hit and Miss* in which the pieces were cut into uniform size and shape but still without regard for color or material because there was not enough of any one kind to carry through. The next step in the growth of design was to sort the colors and arrange them in rows. This produced the *Roman Stripe*. Here, all patches of light value were sewed together into one strip and all those of dark value were sewed into another strip. Then these blocks were pieced together so that there would be alternation of light and dark stripes throughout the quilt. The next variety of rectangular one piece quilt was the checkerboard *Brick Wall*. In this design the strips were sewed in such a way that the joining of two blocks came directly below the center of the rectangular piece above it. The effect was that of a brick wall. There was fine opportunity here for an interesting use of color and texture, the shape being constantly the same. Another one piece design was the *Honey Comb* which started the many mosaic patterns. This was made up of a series of squares with the corners cut off making hexagons.

Real design started, however, when some venturesome quiltmaker cut a rectangle diagonally across the corner. This offered a complexity of design beyond that suggested by the material and provided the opportunity for an interesting arrangement of dark and light. Out of these pieces grew the many variations of diamonds and stars. This group is known as the two piece series of designs and include such quilts as *Flying Birds*, *Birds in Air* and *Flock of Geese*. All the varieties of herringbone designs come in this classification.

The original three piece design was called the *Roman Square* and consisted simply of three rectangles of different colors. These rectangles were usually long and narrow. Many more interesting geometric designs followed. Indeed, the women who made these certainly had to learn their mathematics. The four patch was the square of two. The nine patch was the square of three and on upward to the huge assortment of multiple patterns that were made. The choice of colors for these geometric designs, of which, incidentally, about ninety percent of the old pieced quilts were comprised, was an important factor in the success of the quilts. In the oldest quilts, color was used without consideration of tonal quality because the material was already dyed and the quilt maker had to use whatever she had at hand.

As time went on and new materials could be purchased at reasonable cost, the quilt designer began to choose her color scheme more deliberately. As a result her artistic sense was given ample opportunity of expression and there was found to be no end to the ideas and contrivances to which she would resort for the creation of something original. If any ordinary layman would now work out a huge star with its many hundreds of parts he would indeed appreciate the ingenuity and skill of these early quilt makers.

The separate tiny pieces of a pieced quilt were joined together by a seam. Because of the nature of this technique, straight lines were more general. This form of quilt making was the fundamental one in America and it differed from the quilts of other countries. One pieced quilt is supposed to have had thirty thousand pieces sewed together. These pieces were one-fourth of an inch wide and three fourths of an inch long.

Unfortunately, the verbs to "piece" and to "patch" have been used for the same process but this really should not be so. To piece means to join by means of a sewed seam; to patch means to sew a smaller piece of cloth on a larger one. It is thereby applied—hence the word applique. Before 1750, nearly all quilts were pieced, but from this time on the *Applique Quilt* gained favor. This type is made by laying a small patch on a larger piece, in sections or blocks, and then hemming these down by means of small close stitches. It is apt to be a more complete expression of the quilter's craft because it is created out of whole cloth cut to fit into a particular planned design. There is greater freedom in this method, for the designer is not bound by any precise size, shape, or color of her block. In applique, with a wider range of chosen materials at her command, she can be just as abstract as she desires. A wonderful field in pictorial organization, that is, in space and color relationships is offered here, with all the elements and principles of art structure that go into the composition of a painting.

Because these fundamentals were often overlooked, many very badly designed applique quilts have been made and are still being made. This is due partly to the fact that the early designers were not trained in matters of color and form and only those who had an inherent sense of design were successful from this point of view. It is remarkable, however, under the circumstances, how many finely composed designs were made with a feeling for proportion of line and space and distribution of color.

While we have the applique technique in review, it might be well to consider some of the basic points in art structure upon which a well-designed quilt of this type was made. First, the designer considered the purpose of the quilt—as a bed covering. She then looked at the piece as a whole unit of design and planned the general arrangement of shapes and colors. If a single block was to be used, a large design was usually made for the center. If many blocks were to be used, their arrangement, geometrical or otherwise, was organized and the predominant colors established. From there on each detail was worked out according to the materials and colors to be used.

The different blocks in an *Applique Quilt* were generally set together with strips of material. In the case of a single block, which was usually large enough to form the entire center of the quilt, strips and various borders were joined together, one by one, until the required size was obtained. This kind of quilt was organized in much the same way as an oriental rug. A prayer rug, for instance, consisted of the main design in the center with patterned borders of various sizes surrounding it. There was endless choice of details and shapes. For instance, the center block might be square or elongated, made up of wide or narrow strips of plain colored material or that of variegated design. Because there was never any set design and no actual pattern that had to be followed, no two applique quilts were ever exactly alike in design, coloring or material, though, very broadly speaking, they followed certain traditions in the earlier days. Later on, such traditions were often departed from altogether and fussy designs and elaborate naturalistic renderings made their appearance that were not in good taste.

Among the very many traditional types of design which recur in applique are the *Cockscomb* and the *Princess Feather*. Most often these were made from red and yellow green calicoes. The rose was one of the favorite designs and the *Whig Rose* and the *Democrat Rose* or the *Rose of 1840* are well known.

One of the most used devices in applique was the four block center. In many of the old quilts these blocks were one yard square. Sometimes they were joined simply together so that the four designs formed the center. A good example of this is the *Cherry Tree and Birds* (Page 112). The center is marked by a scalloped design with a floral center. Actually, the design would have been stronger if the little birds flying into the cherry tree had been used as a center design instead. The grape vine is interestingly used here as a running border.

The *Princess Feather*, appliqued in green and plain turkey red calico is an example of the four-block quilt. In this quilt the blocks are joined by small pieces sewed together in the *Cat Track* design. The applique border is interesting with its deep scallops. In this quilt the background quilting is the shell design, and in the corners a leaf pattern is used.

The *Slashed Star* is a very fine example of the quilt which was designed with a border. In this quilt the four blocks are pieced, but the border is applique. The very fine quilting has a center design of rosette and leaves. Graceful flower sprays are quilted into the plain areas.

Another four-block quilt is *The Forest.* This design consists of four oak trees with four leaves and an eight-petaled daisy in the center. A border of oak trees completes the quilt. The quilting is in diagonals forming diamonds with leaf sprays.

Some quilts had five blocks of applique set together with plain blocks. An interesting example of this is the *Charter Oak.* However, in this quilt a small single oak tree was placed in the plain block. This same oak tree appears again in the border with the patriotic eagle. The quilt is made of blue and brown copperplate.

Another example of five blocks, with design alternating with plain blocks, is the *Peony.* The peony is figured green and plain red calico. The border is a tulip with serrated leaves.

DOCUMENT QUILTS

The *Circuit Rider* quilt is an interesting one and comes under the heading of applique, also of the *Album Quilts.* It was made for the one hundred mile circuit in the Western Reserve. It has been said that no matter how stormy the weather nor how difficult the roads, this dauntless preacher astride his chestnut mare carried the message of hope and cheer to his widely scattered country parishioners gathered together in their crossroad churches. He served not only one community but six. He was a man of sound counsel in spiritual and worldly matters. So great was his influence in his wide territory that even today his name is well known and revered in Ohio, and his stories are an important contribution to the folklore of his state.

As a sincere expression of their deep appreciation of his remarkable services, forty women of the United Brethren Church at Miami, Ohio, made him a quilt and presented it to him in 1862. Each woman made her own block and signed her name to it.

Another *Album Quilt* is the pink and white example made for the Reverend Andrew Jackson Bigelow, a Methodist Minister of Central Michigan. A number of women parishioners each contributed a block. The sunburst was the design for the pieced block and in each corner in fine writing in India ink, a woman has signed her name and sometimes the name of her husband and daughter. The *Album* or *Autograph Quilts* have often been used in proving signatures. The story goes that one ambitious woman became a member of the D.A.R. after discovering the signature of her ancestor in an old quilt.

A very important and interesting *Document Quilt* is the *Mary Woodman Washington Map Quilt.* It is about seven and a half by eight feet in size. The top consists of two strips of linen upon which is printed seven copies of the original map of the City of Washington, D. C. When Mary Woodman made this quilt, little did she know that one day her quilt would be used as evidence in the controversy as to who made the first map of the city of Washington. In this copperplate quilt Major Andrew Ellicott, the Pennsylvania Quaker, drew the plans and mapped the city with the official backing and sanction of George Washington. The linen is coarse homespun and the map is printed from a copperplate in a red-brown color. It is believed that only eight printings were made on the linen and seven of these are in the Mary Woodman quilt. From family records it is found that the printed linen was given to Mary by her father, Captain Samuel Woodman, on her sixteenth birthday. Captain Woodman was in command of a full rigged ship trading in American and foreign ports and while loading his cargo in Philadelphia, he came into possession of the linen with the copperplate printing of the Washington map.

A portrait of George Washington is in an oval design in the upper left corner with the legend: "George Washington, President of the United States." This homespun linen was printed three years before Stuart painted his famous portrait of the President. In the top right corner appears the crest of the Washington family. It shows three stars and two horizontal stripes surmounted by an open Bible; also the initial *W* followed by the word "Sculptor." Under this is the inscription, "Plan of the City of Washington in the Territory of Columbia ceded by the States of Virginia and Maryland to the United States of America and by them established as the seat of their Government after the year M D C C C." In the lower left corner, etched in old colonial style, is a description (under the title of "Observations Explanatory of the Plan") of the proposed positions of streets and buildings. Printed on the fabric are the words: "the plan is by Mr. Ellicott."

Major Ellicott fought in the Revolutionary War and is one of the five Revolutionary soldiers to be buried at the United States Military Academy at West Point. Mary Woodman, born at South Hampton, New Hampshire in 1796, made the map quilt from the linen strips in 1814. The family moved in a wagon driven by an oxteam to Cornville, Maine, a little town (now Skowhegan) in 1831. The quilt was among the household goods they took with them, but for sixty-four years it was almost forgotten by its owners. This historically important map quilt is owned by Dr. Ephraim R. Hackett of Chesterville, Maine. It was on display for an entire year in the Library of Congress during the Washington Bi-Centennial in 1932.

In American literature it is interesting to note how often in a story of country life mention was made of quilts. Mrs. Wiggs of cabbage patch fame said: "Piecing quilts was keepin' at peace and doin' away with the scraps." Aunt Jane of Kentucky said: "There is a heap of comfort in making quilts, just to sit and sort over the pieces and call to mind this piece or that is the dress of a loved friend."

PART SIX

QUILTING

QUILTING FRAMES

After the tops of the quilts were completed and each tiny piece of colored material was sewed into place, the process of quilting was ready to be started. The best way to quilt a top was to stretch it on a frame. This frame was so simple and so inexpensive that every household possessed its own. The frame consisted of four poles or pieces of board, usually pine, about two or three inches wide, one or two inches thick and nine feet long. These strips of wood had pieces of heavy homespun muslin, or ticking, tacked along their entire length. They were fastened at the four corners with metal clamps.

The back of the quilt was fastened to the frame by basting, or by means of pins. Over this was spread the filling which might be cotton, wool, "flock," or a thin worn wool blanket. The decorative top was carefully stretched over this. Great care was used in placing the top because it had to be extremely smooth with no gatherings or fullness of any kind.

DESIGNS FOR QUILTING

In studying the old quilts it is interesting to see how fine was the taste of the quilters. Great reserve was shown in the choice of pattern. In the backgrounds to quilts where there was a great deal of design in the colored blocks, simple all-over designs were used, such as the shell. The quickest background pattern, and perhaps the easiest to make was the diagonal. Diagonal quilting was much more effective than the horizontal or vertical quilting following the weave of the material. Single diagonal lines arranged in groups formed patterns called double and triple diagonals. When diagonals running in the opposite direction crossed, diamonds were formed. When the diagonals were unequally spaced, the resulting designs were called *Hanging Diamonds* or *Broken Plaid.*

When there were open spaces in the blocks or in the corners, design units were used such as *Princess Wreaths*, *Cornucopias*, *Harps*, *Pineapples*, *Stars*, *Peacock Fans*, *Oak Leaves*, *Swirls*, *Birds*, *Starfish*, *Circles*, *Spider Web*, *Weeping Willow*, *Rosettes*, *Comet*, *Bouquet*, *Dove of Peace*, *Eagles*. Various designs were also used in the colored pieces of the quilts and flowers and flower wreaths were perhaps the most popular. In the borders, running vines were used. A favorite design for the border was the *Cable*, *Princess Feather*, the *Serpentine*, and the *Ocean Wave*.

The sources of design for quilting were the same as for the units which formed the blocks for the tops. Religious motifs were used, such as harps and crosses. Patriotic emblems appeared in corners such as eagles, anchors, flags and liberty bells.

Perhaps there was more originality in the borders than anywhere else in the quilt. Vines wound around half-pilasters, showing that the quilt artist may have been influenced by wall-papers, low relief plaster, or the carved wood of mantels, bedsteads, chests or stencilled chairs. The delicate wreaths and medallions used by the Adam brothers appeared in quilting designs. At times these wreaths encircled flowers. At other times sunbursts centered the quilts and fans finished the corners. For the quilter the designs suggested by the furniture maker had to be simplified. Urns were transformed into baskets. Sunbursts and quarter-fans helped to break large uninteresting areas and gave an added interest to corners. Nature forms, such as oak leaves and acorns, pine cones and pineapples appeared in painted and carved dower chests. These were made into single motifs and sometimes were put into trailing vines for borders of quilts. Geometric designs were used with a crudely drawn spray of foliage, a heart, a disc, or a circle. Hearts were usually to be found in the quilting on a bride's quilt. Bells not only connoted patriotism but also the gaiety and happiness of a wedding, hence bells are often found in bride's quilts.

Strange as it may seem, quilts were sometimes made from old dresses worn by thrifty quilters in deep mourning. The quilts of the Civil War were made of black, gray, and brown calicoes, and in the quilting one may find the *Weeping Willow*. The morbidity in these women which found expression in mourning pictures, hair and wax flower wreaths, samplers and quilts is reflected in the poem "The Patchwork Quilt" by Natalie Whitted.

MARKING THE PATTERN

When the pattern was decided upon, there were several techniques for the application of the design to the quilt. A spur was sometimes used which did the work of the dressmaker's wheel. Some quilt makers used a string fastened tightly to the sides of the quilt. White chalk was run along this string and snapped. In this way a straight line was made on the quilt which could be easily erased. The popular story is that in some communities a bride was allowed only to snap her *Bride's Quilt*. All the rest of the quilting was done by her friends.

In applying patterns for the quilting to the tops, often a template was made from stiff paper, cardboard or buckram. A line was drawn around this with starch or chalk, pencil and charred pointed sticks being rarely used because they soiled the quilts.

There is a decided art to quilting, and though each woman developed her own technique, there had always to be an evenness of stitch and a certain regularity of touch which would become rhythmical once the work was started. It is no easy thing to take short, even stitches through three thicknesses of cloth. Knots could not show and no fastening of threads were to be visible. The whole quilt had to be one mass of short, even stitches. The very position in which the work was done made even stitches difficult. The left hand had to be held under the work while the right plied the needle, and great care had to be taken so that no fingers were pricked, for the tiniest drop of blood would stain the quilt.

ALL WHITE QUILTS

Perhaps the finest and now the rarest of all quilts is the *All White* quilt which depended upon the fine quilting alone for its success. These quilts were made of homespun cotton or linen and were most elaborately executed. There was usually a large center medallion with a series of borders around it. Many times the center medallion contained an urn or a basket of flowers surrounded by an elaborate border of *Princess Feathers*. In these *All White* quilts the reverse side was quite as lovely as the top. Indeed, in imitation of these meticulously quilted counterpanes (white quilts were invariably used as spreads) came the machine made Marseilles spreads. But fine as they were, they never could replace the handmade *All White* quilts.

The stuffed quilt was another form of quilting. This was much like trapunto which came to America from Italy. The pattern was pricked, and in the little pocket-like portion of the design, cotton was pulled or stuffed in. A quilter who was expert enough with her needle to do this, also made cordings in her quilting. Rolls of cotton were sewed in rows in the quilts. Many times the skilled person who made the quilt also sewed in the elaborate patterns herself so that her careful fingers stuffed her design evenly. She then was willing to have her friends help her with the background.

Many of the old *All White* quilts show dark spots and these are the cotton seeds which were not ginned out. In the South particularly, home grown cotton found its way, seeds and all, into the early quilts. It is difficult and quite unauthentic, however, to date quilts by these seeds. Some collectors say that every quilt showing seeds predates the cotton gin of 1790.

This, however, is not altogether true, because many quilt makers in Tennessee, Alabama, Mississippi and Louisiana, filled their quilts with the cotton grown on their own places. The cotton of the wealthy planters was especially free from seeds for the children of the negro slaves would pick them out by hand. In other cotton growing communities the seeds were not so carefully picked out because there was not the same cheap labor to do it.

THE QUILTING BEE

The function of the *Quilting Bee* was not only to offer opportunity to the ambitious quilt maker to get her quilting done for the season, but it was the most important social event of the neighborhood. It was far more refined and "genteel" than other gatherings such as the "apple paring," "cornhusking" or the "thrashing," because to it the guests could wear their best Sunday clothes. This was an important consideration as there were so few gala occasions upon which these clothes could, in fact, be worn. During the long months when the piecing or patching of the quilt was in progress, everyone looked forward to the *Quilting Bee*. It was the most popular form of feminine hospitality and the best quilters were always invited. Since fine needlework was requisite to admission it behooved every socially inclined woman to be very expert with her needle. If the hostess found that one quilter varied her stitches the slightest degree, another job was found for her, probably in the kitchen where the huge dinner was being prepared for the evening when the men arrived and stayed a while before they took their wives home. At this time, games were also played and there was much dancing and singing. Around this merrymaking Stephen C. Foster wrote *The Quilting Party:*

> "*In the sky the bright stars glittered*
> *On the banks the pale moon shone,*
> *And 'twas from Aunt Dinah's Quilting Party,*
> *I was seeing Nellie home.*"

There was another side to the quilting party which certainly must not be overlooked and this was the opportunity it offered for exchange of confidences or gossip. When the twelve women—arranged three on a side of the quilt frame—started out to quilt, they were wide apart; indeed, they were nine feet apart. But as the sides were rolled up, they came closer and closer together until, when the quilt was finished, they were face to face. The conversation would be very general when the quilt was started—the crops and the weather were safe subjects, also politics which, as we see, actually entered into the names of quilts. At first the talk was loud enough to be heard by all but as the quilters came closer and closer together, the conversation became correspondingly more intimate. Small events were magnified and many an individual reputation was made or marred.

A very interesting description of a quilting party in the South appears in "*Suwannee River*" by Cecile Hulse Matschat, in the chapter "Quiltin' Kivers." A lengthy piece is quoted as it gives us the real flavor of these functions and a picture of the people, the houses and the food which was served.

"The first guest had arrived; the big room in the new addition house buzzed with chatter as they laid their stiffly ironed sunbonnets carefully on the high bed and hunted out their scissors and thimbles from the deep pockets of their cotton and calico frocks. This was womernfowkses doin's. No men were allowed. The women gazed about them in awe and envy. Manthy was a master hand for smartin' up. Even the homemade furniture looked better than the store chairs they had saved for months to own. There were straight-backed pine chairs, made more than a generation ago, with legs stubbed from wear on the puncheon floor, and pieced cushions of cotton tied on the seats. The bed of sweet gum in the corner still cast off a faint fragrance from its hardened aromatic sap. Over the cords, which took the place of springs, was a double mattress of softened corn husks and a feather bed of the finest and downiest goose feathers covered with soft cotton sheets and pieced quilts. The top spread, in gay reds, blues, and greens was Cella's favorite pattern, the *Double Wedding Ring*. The cypress chest beneath the window held Cella's personal things, collected against the day when she would leave the homesite for a place of her own.

"Manthy stood on a chair in the big room, hanging heavy cords from hooks to suspend the quilting frames at the proper height, so that the women could quilt while sitting down, two to a side and one on each end. The floor has been freshly swept, and two quilt linings of heavy dyed unbleached muslin were spread out, ready for the smooth layers of cotton that would serve as fillers.

"Two patchwork covers were spread wide and placed over the cotton-covered lining on the floor, edge to edge, and basted into place. Hundreds of little pieces were sewed together with fine stitches to form a pattern. The top for the green lining was the *Snake Fence* pattern, in shades of yellow and pinkish brown; the other cover was *Joseph's Coat*, and certainly every type of color and patch was represented. Before her dazzled eyes were spread dozens of others, to be quilted up during the long winter nights. The names were enchanting: *Wild Goose Chase*, *Lover's Knot*, *Buzzard's Roost*, *Star of the East*, *Log Cabin*, *Strangers*, *Bird of Paradise*, *Cherokee Rose*, *Odds and Ends*, *Patience*, *Widow's Troubles*, *Forbidden Fruit*, *Hen and Chicken*—and each was different from any of the rest.

"The side frames were laid beside each quilt, then the end pieces were bound on with stout cord and the quilts stretched into shape, with the ends firmly fastened. As soon as the quilts swung from the cords, the women pulled up their chairs and started to sew, six to a quilt, using fine even stitches through the top, cotton and lining, and following the agreed pattern.

"After dinner, work went smoothly and well. The talk was all of women's doin's—of death, of sickness, of signs and portents, and of the everyday happenings of their lives."

There is another interesting description which helps to round out our impression of the *Quilting Bee* in the different communities. The following notes are taken from a letter giving an account of an 1840 bee in Lancaster County, Pennsylvania: "On the table were beef-steaks, boiled pork, sweet potatoes, 'Kohl Slaw,' pickled cucumbers and red beets, apple butter and preserved peaches, pumpkin and apple pie, sponge cake and coffee. After dinner came our next neighbors (Pennsylvania Dutch), Susy and Katy Groff, who live in single blessedness and great neatness. The farmer's wife wore hoops, and was of the 'world's people.' All spoke Dutch for the Groffs do not speak English with fluency yet."

"The first subject of conversation was the fall housecleaning. Such terms as: 'Die carpet hinaus an der fence,' 'Die Fenshter und die porch,' 'My goodness, es was schlim' were heard throughout the conversation (half English and half German).

"We quilted, rolled, talked, laughed, got one quilt done and put in another. The work wasn' fine (she wanted her quilting done in a hurry) and we laid it out by chalking around a small plate. At five o'clock we had supper (stewed chicken and plenty of it, coffee, etc.). Then some of the husbands arrived to call for some of the wives and take them home. Some of us continued by candle light, and we got the second quilt done by 7:00. As we got ready to go home, I showed my new alpaca and dyed merino and the new Philadelphia bonnet which exposes the back of my head (my dear!) to the wint'ry blast. We parted with invitations to visit."

After the strenuous activity of the *Quilting Bee* was over the tired hostess would, the following day, cut the threads which held her quilt to the frames and she would then bind the edges of the quilt. Usually a bias piece of the cotton was used. Sometimes this was white, sometimes it was the predominating printed calico of the pattern. This quilt was then placed on the shelf or in the blanket chest ready for the first cold night.

PART SEVEN

CONCLUSION

As we have seen earlier, the art of making a pieced quilt was just one of the occupations the early housewife indulged in during her rare periods of rest. Between cooking, cleaning house, milking the cows, churning butter, helping on the farm, spinning and weaving cloth, making clothes for the family and curtains and bedspreads, hooking or weaving rugs, and being just plain mother, her task was enormous—from the early days of colonization through the Civil War.

At about this time, however, modern industrialism began in earnest and women, as well as men, started to leave the farms and the rural areas for the factories of the towns and cities. What happened then to the home crafts, not only in America but everywhere in the Western world? A few of the old craftsmen remained, mostly in small towns and rural areas, but their products were no longer valued as they used to be. In one or two of the fine arts schools of this country, for instance, directors told their students that the machine was man's best friend and that it was old-fashioned to work with the hands when things could be made so much more quickly mechanically. With this type of thinking, the average American lost much of his respect for handwork.

Many people still do believe, however, that creative hands can help make the balance between material advance and social progress—probably many more people than outwardly it appears. And happily, in recent years, there has been a renaissance in American folk art. The start was made way back by the study and collection of the work of the native Indians. Each piece was looked at from an historical point of view, and rather as an individual curiosity. Then the interest grew in how each piece was designed. This interest spread to local historical societies and museums who accumulated interesting collections of *all* early American folk art and exhibited them as examples of native design. Old glass became a vogue and as people searched their attics all sorts of hidden treasures presented themselves and were restored. The interest in Americana spread rapidly and steadily. Private collectors began to exhibit their best pieces, the American wings of the museums throughout the country assumed greater importance and the fashion for home decorating in modified versions of "Early American" became the order of the day.

During recent years, the finest recognition of the folk art of America has been given by the government sponsored Index of American Design, with headquarters now at the National Gallery in Washington. This is a record largely made up of water color renderings of native objects of art as well as clothing, shoes, even tools and implements, figureheads and some ships. Many of these have great beauty but, above all *say* what this country is.

We still find today in America, craftsmen and artists, among whom, of course, are the quilt makers, working quietly at home. The main difference between these people and their forefathers is that they have been liberated from much drudgery of housework by the machine. To what extent this comparative feeling of leisure, the lack of urgency affects the characteristics of their work will be judged in years to come, but the same desire exists among today's craftsmen to express themselves in a useful way and to derive the satisfaction of achievement that only hand craftsmanship can give.

Wherever there are quilt makers the feeling is much like that of "Aunt Jane of Kentucky" when she said: "You see you start out with just so much caliker; you don't go to the store and pick it out and buy it, but the neighbors will give you a piece here and a piece there, and you will have a piece left every time you cut out a dress, and you take just what happens to come and that's predestination. But when it comes to cuttin' out why you're free to choose your patterns. You can give the same kind o' pieces to two persons, and one will be a *Nine Patch* and one'll make a *Wild Goose Chase* and there'll be two quilts made out o' the same kind of pieces, and jest as different as they can be, and that is just the way with livin'. The Lord sends us the pieces, but we can cut 'em out and put 'em together pretty much to suit ourselves, and there's a heap in the cuttin' out and sewin' then there is in the caliker."

And Nathaniel Hawthorne must have had quilts or quilting in mind when in the *Marble Faun* he wrote these lines:

"There is something extremely pleasant, and even touching—at least, or a very sweet, soft and winning effect—in this peculiarity of needlework, distinguishing women from men. Our own sex is incapable of any such by-play aside from the main business of life, but women—be they of what earthly rank they may, however gifted with intellect or genius, or endowed with awful beauty—have always some little handiwork ready to fill the gap of every vacant moment. A needle is familiar to fingers of them all. A queen, no doubt, plies it on occasions; the woman-poet can use it as adroitly as her pen; the woman's eye, that has discovered a new star, turns from its glory to send the polished little instrument gleaming along the hem of her kerchief, or to darn a casual fray in her dress. And they have greatly the advantage of us in this respect. The slender thread of silk or cotton keeps them united with the small, familiar, gentle interests of life, the continually operating influence of which do so much for the health of the character, and carry off what would otherwise be a dangerous accumulation of morbid sensibility. A vast deal of human sympathy runs along this electric line, stretching from the throne to the wicker chair of the humblest seamstress, and keeping high and low in a species of communion with their kindred beings. Methinks it is a token of healthy and gentle characteristics, when women of high thoughts and accomplishments love to sew; especially as they are never more at home with their own hearts than while so occupied.

"And when the work falls in a woman's lap, of its own accord, and the needle involuntarily ceases to fly, it is a sign of trouble, quite as trustworthy as the throb of the heart itself."

In conclusion let us repeat Hawthorne by saying that women still are "never more at home with their own hearts" than while they are sewing. In farmhouses in the country, in cabins on the windswept plains, in fine houses surrounded by gardens, in apartments in cities, they are still carrying on this art of the American people. They venture into the difficulties and happy surprises of making their own designs. Like their grandmothers and great-grandmothers, they make pictorial use of their own familiar surroundings and their pets. However, they no longer work only with scraps "left over," but with all the wealth of materials and color that America today has at their command.

(*Metropolitan Museum of Art*)

"Les Plaisirs de la Ferme." A Toile de Jouy cotton print designed by J. B. Huet between 1785-1790.

(Metropolitan Museum of Art)

Above: An early example of American printed cotton (1700-1750), woven at Bound Brook, New Jersey. Below: "William Henry Harrison Campaign," a later American printed cotton made in the nineteenth century in brown on white. Opposite page, top: "The Fall of the Bastille" from a printed cotton piece signed "Gordon, sculpt." (English, c. 1850). Opposite page, bottom left: "Les Travaux de la Manufacture," a Toile de Jouy copperplate print made at Oberkampf, about 1784. Opposite page bottom right: "The Marriage of Figaro." Another Toile de Jouy copperplate print made between 1794-1800 and designed by J. B. Huet.

(Metropolitan Museum of Art)

Institute of Chicago)

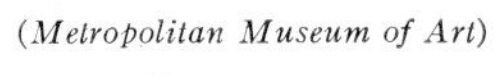
(Metropolitan Museum of Art)

(*Metropolitan Museum of Art*)

"Les Delices des Quatre Saisons." A Toile de Jouy copperplate print, designed by J. B. Huet at Jouy, about 1785.

"La Marchande d'Amour." A Toile de Jouy copperplate print designed by Hippolyte Lebas at Jouy, about 1817.

(Metropolitan Museum of Art)

"Le Loup et l'Agneau." Another Toile de Jouy copperplate print, designed by J. B. Huet and made in 1804.

(Metropolitan Museum of Art)

(Edison Museum, Dearborn)

An older example of Toile de Jouy with allegorical scenes, made in France in the eighteenth century.

(*Art Institute of Chicago*)

Above: Section of an "Indiennes" French block printed cotton, made at Bordeaux or Nantes, about 1770. Right: A nineteenth century English printed cotton in a tan chintz with all-over peony design. Opposite page: A printed interlaced design on red cotton ground, made about 1787 in Nantes, France.

(*Art Institute of Chicago*)

(Art Institute of Chicago)

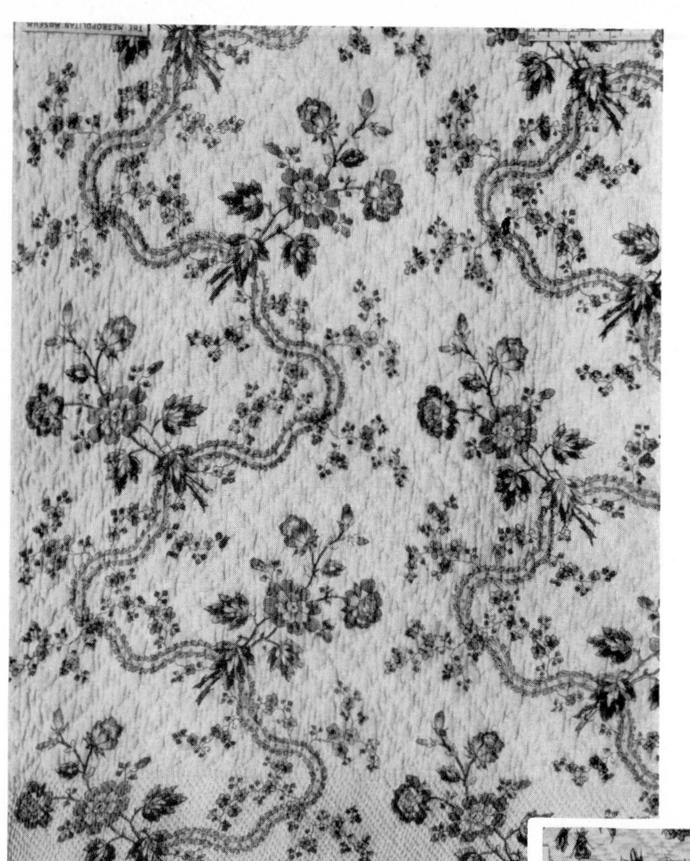

Fragment of a quilted skirt in "Toil Peinte," with delicate design similar i feeling to a wall paper. French 1783-1789

(*Metropolitan Museum of Art*)

Opposite page: A typical example of a French "Chinoiserie" copperplate cotton design in the style of Pillement.

(*Metropolitan Museum of Art*)

Right: Detail of a Polychrome quilt in hand painted cotton, made in France between 1783-1790.

(*Edison Museum, Dearborn*)

(Art Institute of Chicago)

The famous "Doctor Syntax" design (which also appeared on dinner plates) printed on cotton in England during the eighteenth century.

(*Art Institute of Chicago*)

Left: Eighteenth century French cotton print. The repeated design of the boy with a dog, and the girl with a cat, among foliage, garlands of flowers and draperies, is printed on a red ground. Below: "La Trêve de Dieu." A French cotton of about 1810, also printed on a plain ground.

(*Art Institute of Chicago*)

(Edison Museum, Dearborn)

(Art Institute of Chicago)

Above: "L'Agreable Leçon," a late eighteenth or early nineteenth century printed French cotton. Right: "La Trêve de Dieu," another French printed cotton made in Alsace about 1820.

(Art Institute of Chicago)

(Art Institute of Chicago)

Above and right: Two more versions of "La Trêve de Dieu" in printed cotton, made at Jouy about 1820.

Left: A two-tone cylinder cotton print with Victorian design made in England about 1850.

(Metropolitan Museum of Art)

(*Philadelphia Museum of Art*)

(*Metropolitan Museum of Art*)

(Edison Museum, Dearborn)

Opposite page, top and bottom: "Penn's Treaty with the Indians." A piece of material and detail of the design. An English made cotton print (c. 1800). Above: "Courtship and Marriage" in Toile de Jouy and Right: a French printed cotton design with medallions of Eros, doves, flower baskets on a red ground, made about 1810.

(Art Institute of Chicago)

(*Art Institute of Chicago*)

Opposite page, top: "Lafayette," a French copperplate print from Alsace (1825-1830). Opposite page, bottom: "Le Bal," a French printed cotton of about 1825.

(*Metropolitan Museum of Ar*

Above: "Cortez Refuses the Indians' Presents," a French printed cotton made at Nantes or Rouen in 1825. Below: "Apotheosis of Franklin," an English printed cotton of about 1776, in pink on white.

(*Metropolitan Museum of Art*)

(*Art Institute of Chicago*)

CRAZY AND PATCHWORK QUILTS

(*Chicago Historical Society*)

Above. Crazy quilt, by an unknown maker but to which the following information is attached: "This crazy quilt my aunt helped piece the squares and I worked all but five of them and painted all these that are painted. We both worked the border. Was made in the year 1878."

Opposite page: Patchwork and chintz applique quilt with a chicken and flower pot design. The varied colored chintz is on a white background. Made about 1800 by Mary Satchwell.

(*Index of American Design*)

(*Index of American Design*)

Above: Crazy quilt with elaborate designs in small squares. Pattern in quilts began to appear in triangular pieces and squar such as these.

Opposite page: An example of "Fanny's Fan" a simple patchwork quilt with organized design.

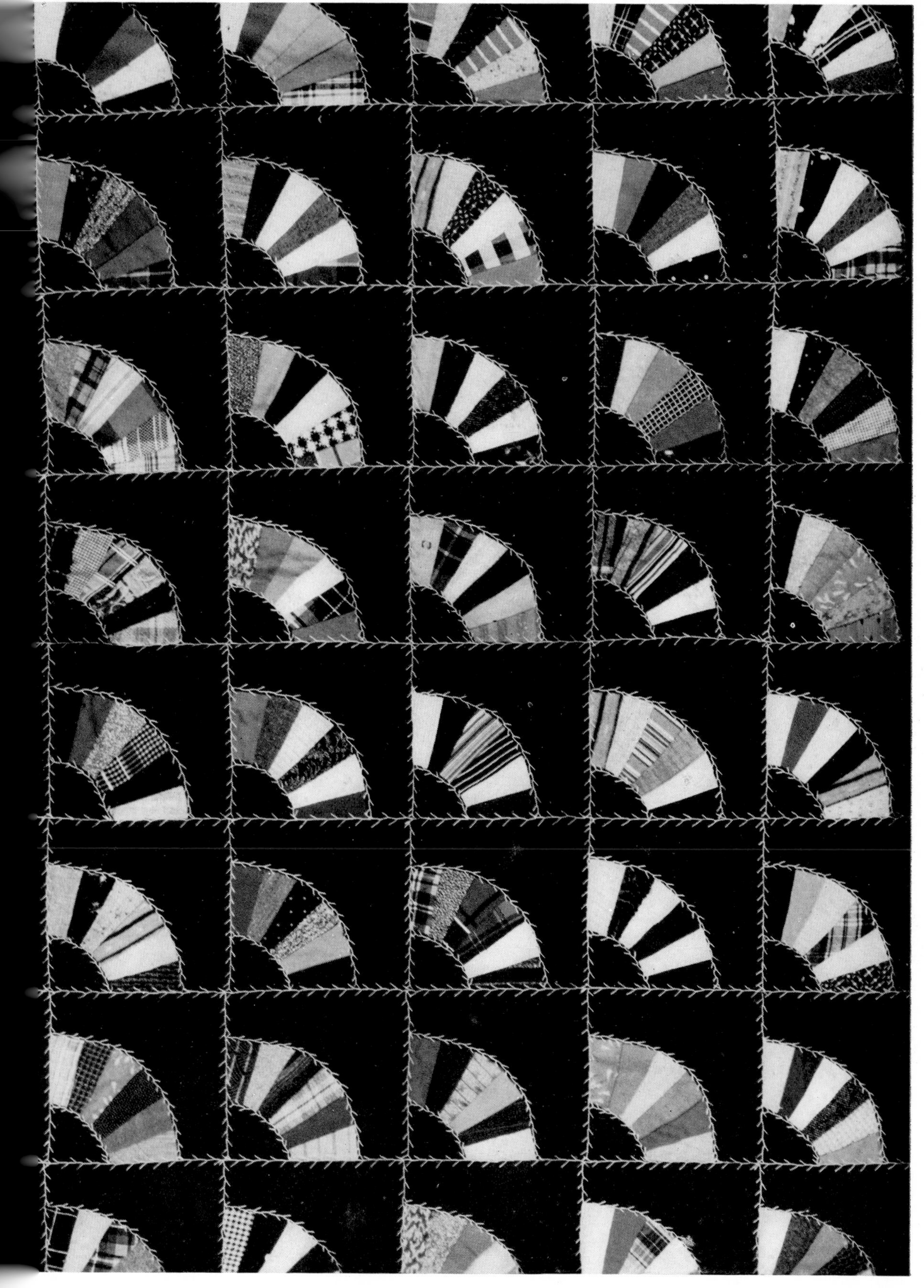

(*Edison Museum, Dearborn*)

(*Courtesy, Charles Weidman*)

Above: Embroidered patchwork quilt in velvet and silk patches with a mosaic-like effect. This was made in 1886 by R Wolcott Hoffman in Sioux City. Opposite page: Patchwork crazy quilt, made in 1899 at St. George, Utah. Notice how names sewn on the quilt help to bring the design together.

(*Courtesy, Miss Mabel Jarvis*)

(Edison Museum, Dearborn)

A splendid example of the hit or miss quilt, made of interesting pieces of copperplate and other color printed cottons.

A very old design with the "Windmill" center and "Hit or Miss" in the rest of the quilt. In the "Hit or Miss" quilts we find organization of the size of the pieces of material used, but little in the arrangement of the material itself as every old piece of printed cotton was used.

(Edison Museum, Dearborn)

(*Brooklyn Museum*)

A fine nineteenth century "Log Cabin" pieced quilt designed with a cross in the center and square bands of different colored cotton materials.

Log cabin pieced quilt in homespun and hard-twilled woolen materials, with a bright red in the center of each block. The quilt was made about 1875 by Mrs. J. Still in Rochester, New York.

(*Index of American Design*)

(*Brooklyn Museum*)

On this page are details from two "Log Cabin" quilts made in the nineteenth century. The "Log Cabin" type of pieced quilt was so called because of the long strips or log-shaped pieces of material used. There is more design in these than on the "Hit or Miss" or, of course in the "Crazy Quilts", examples which appear on preceding pages. Opposite page: Another "Log Cabin" quilt made for a doll's bed in the early nineteenth century.

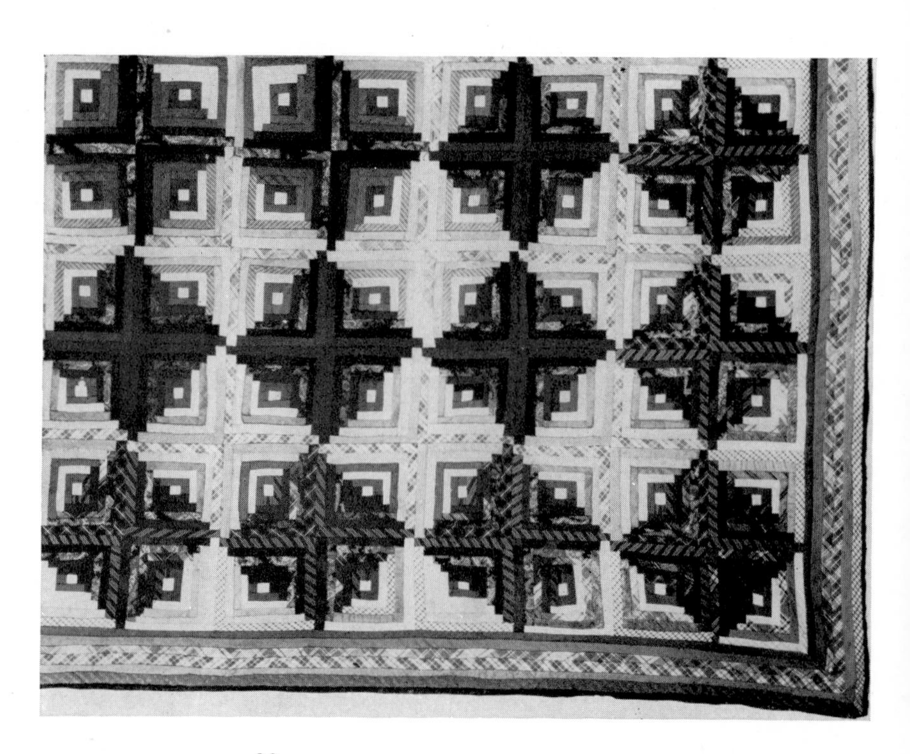

(*Los Angeles Museum*)

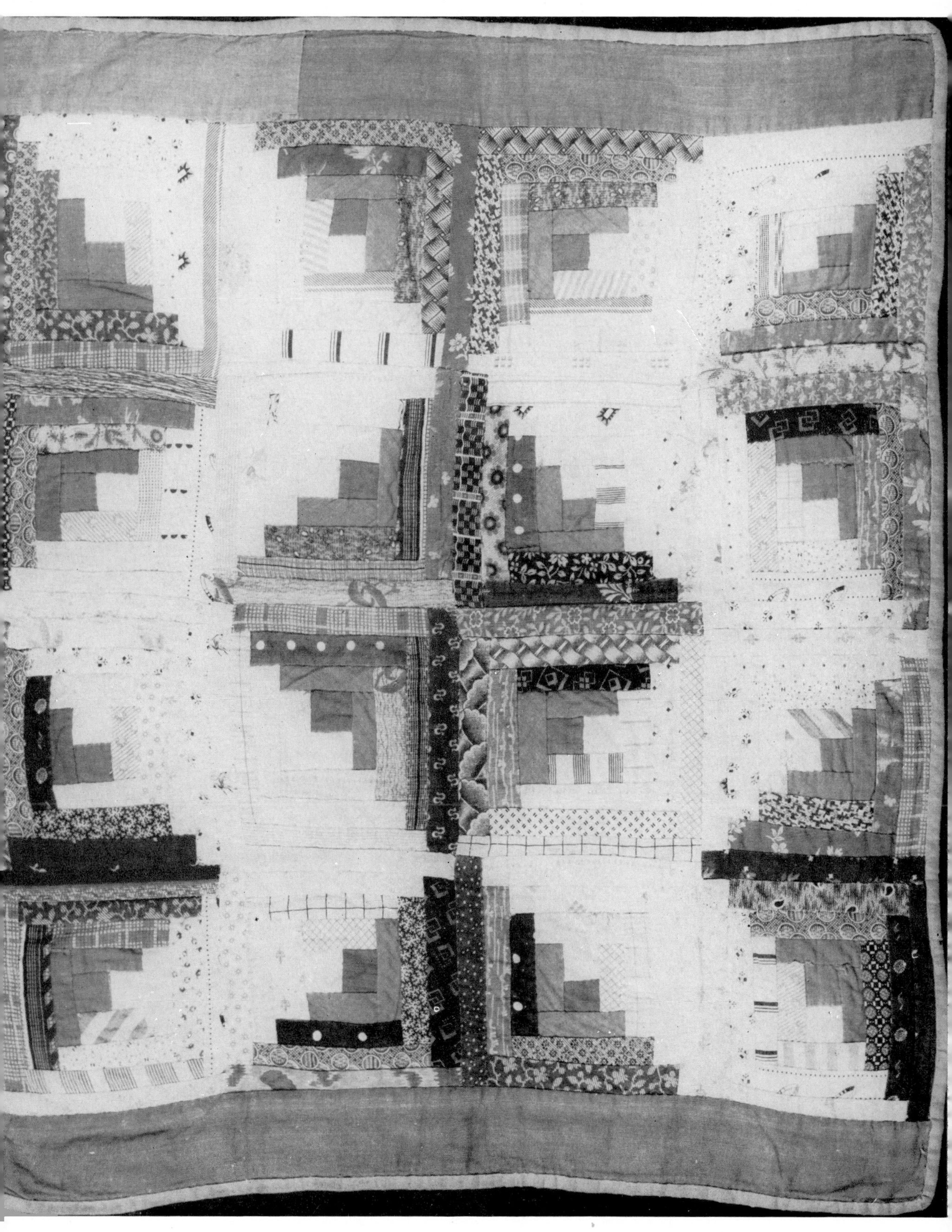

(Brooklyn Museum

(*Index of American Design*)

A multicolored patchwork and applique quilt of chintz and calico, with "Star of Bethlehem" center. It was made about 1812 by the Drake family of Staten Island. The pieced quilts of this category show a real sense of design and craftsmanship. The color and the materials were fully organized into the design.

[A]nother striking "Star of Bethlehem" design ("Rainbow Star") with a total of 1352 pieces in the center star (167 in each of [t]he 8 points). It was made in Lebanon, Pennsylvania, around 1850, and has an air of "Pennsylvania Dutch" about it.

(Index of American Design)

(Courtesy, Mrs. Eleza Vandergraft Sutton)

Above: A beautiful pieced quilt with a variety of different printed materials arranged in octagonal rings of small diamond with a star center and corners, and a border with bird and garlands. Opposite page: A quilt with the "Wheel of Fortune" pattern alternating with quilted blocks each of different design. It was made in 1864, by Betty D. Mann.

(*Courtesy, Mrs. Galloway*)

An unusual pieced quilt of very formal design with an "Eight Pointed Star" in the center, echoed in the oriental carpet-like border. This quilt was made in 1850.

(Philadelphia Museum of Art)

(Courtesy, Mrs. Dora Bennett Taliaferro)

Applique and quilted bedspread made about 1841, at William Bennett Farm, Union County, Indiana. Red, green and yellow calico is sewn in a circular leaf design and in small diamonds, framing the "Sunflower" pattern.

Right: Quilt in the "Star of Bethlehem" pattern made with printed cottons in organized colors and materials. Below: A detail of another "Star of Bethlehem" quilt made around 1835. The quilting in the corners is particularly interesting in this example.

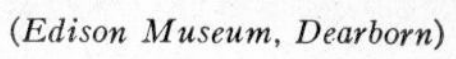

(Edison Museum, Dearborn)

(Philadelphia Museum of Art)

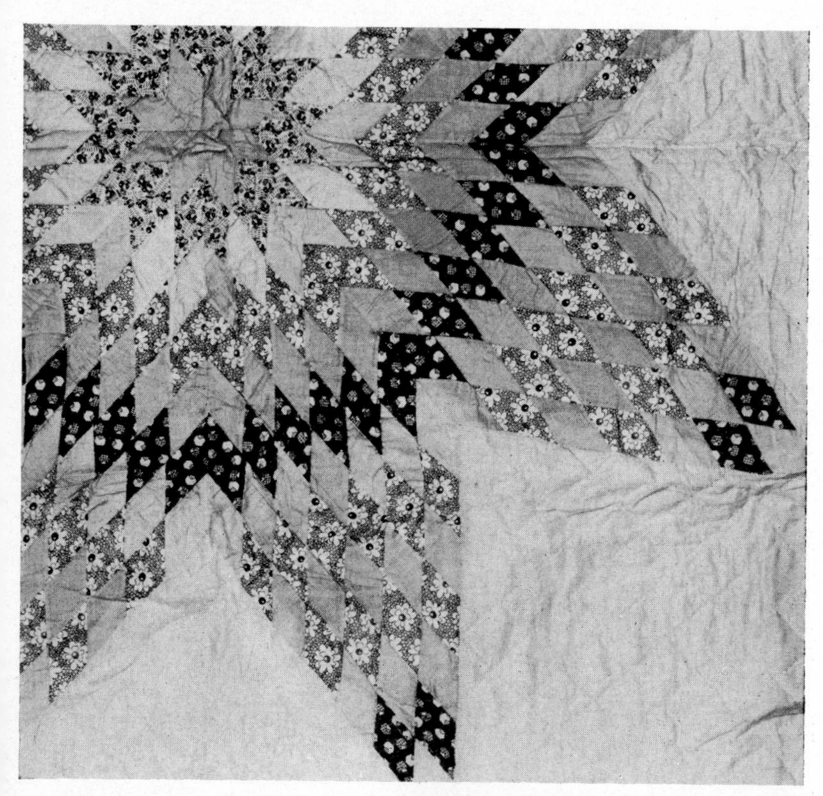

Left: A corner detail of a "Star of Bethlehem" quilt, made of floral printed cottons on a quilted background. Below: A fine old copperplate print is the background of this fourth example of "The Star of Bethlehem" design, made with many interesting pieces of patterned and plain colored calicoes.

(*Edison Museum, Dearborn*)

(*Brooklyn Museum*)

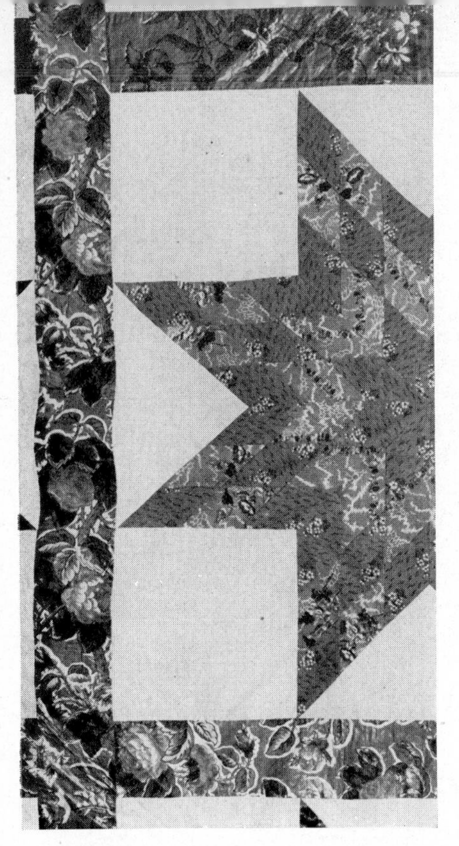

(Author's collection)

Opposite page: Initialled blue and w. tufted and patchworked quilt, with charming arrangement of diagonal-li flower petal design in printed cotton. was made in 1826 by Sarah Parell.

Sections from three blocks in the same quilt, made in Maryland about 1845. Each "Star of Bethlehem" pattern is different in color and material—made up of copperplate prints and glazed chintz.

(*Index of American Design*)

Left: A corner detail of a quilt with the "North Carolina" or "Virginia Lily" pattern in watered yellow and figured green calico. It was made in 1840. Below: Red and green applique quilt on white background with "Lover's Knot" border, also made about 1840, in Maine.

(*Art Institute of Chicago*)

(*Courtesy Mrs. Peggy Wester*)

(Courtesy, Mrs. Grace McKnight)

Calico pieced and appliqued quilt on muslin, with "Lily" pattern in red, blue and white, made in 1835.

(Edison Museum, Dearborn)

Above: Applique quilt in "Wedding Ring" design in different patterned cottons on a plain ground. Left: "Robbing Peter to Pay Paul." An applique quilt in red and white unbleached muslin and calico, cut in geometric design. It was made in Silver Springs, Pennsylvania, about 1836. The examples shown on this and the opposite page are corner details from each quilt.

(Courtesy Mrs. A. C. Myers)

Right: Applique quilt in light blue, yellow and red. The red "Rick Rack" border is pieced—the exquisite quilting has rosettes in the center with a double feather design, while the border has the "Running Feather" motif. Below: "Pincushion and Burrs" or "Square and Swallows." An applique quilt, made in 1830, with "Cat Track" border. The quilting is designed in bunches of grapes.

(*Author's collection*)

(*Art Institute of Chicago*)

(*Art Institute of Chicago*)

Left: Detail of a quilt with "Cherry Basket" or "Flower Basket" pattern, made in 1860, with red calico on plain white. The quilting is in feather rosette design. Below: Another "Flower Basket" design (detail) in orange calico with black dots, made in 1862. The quilting is in squares with feather border. Opposite page, top: Corner of a fine appliqued quilt with "Sunrise Pattern" in cottons of uniform designs and color. Opposite page, bottom: Corner detail of a "Slashed Star" pattern quilt, made in 1840, in applique with vine border. Red, blue, green and yellow figured calico was used. The quilting is in a flower spray design.

(*Art Institute of Chicago*)

(*Courtesy*
Mrs. Belle S. Black)

(*Art Institute of*
Chicago)

(*The Chicago Historical Society*)

Red, white and blue "Diamond Quilt," made by Mrs. Austin Ernest from the linen bunting which decorated the stand from which Abraham Lincoln spoke in Paris, Illinois, September 7, 1858. A four stripe border of the three colors runs around the quilt. The quilting is in long rows which follow the diamond patterns. The border quilting follows the border strips.

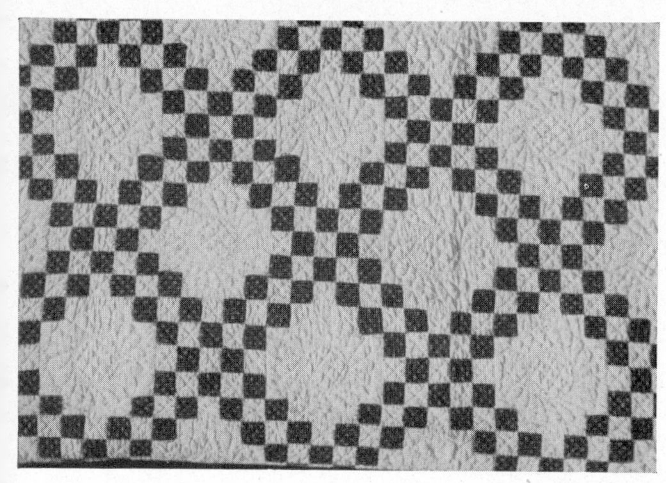

(*Art Institute of Chicago*)

Left: "Double Irish Chain" pattern in blue and orange calico with "Princess Feather" quilting. This applique quilt was made in 1850. Below: A very old example of the "Nine Patch" quilt in various printed cottons. The design is held together by the band of one material that borders each square. (Both are details).

(*Edison Museum, Dearborn*)

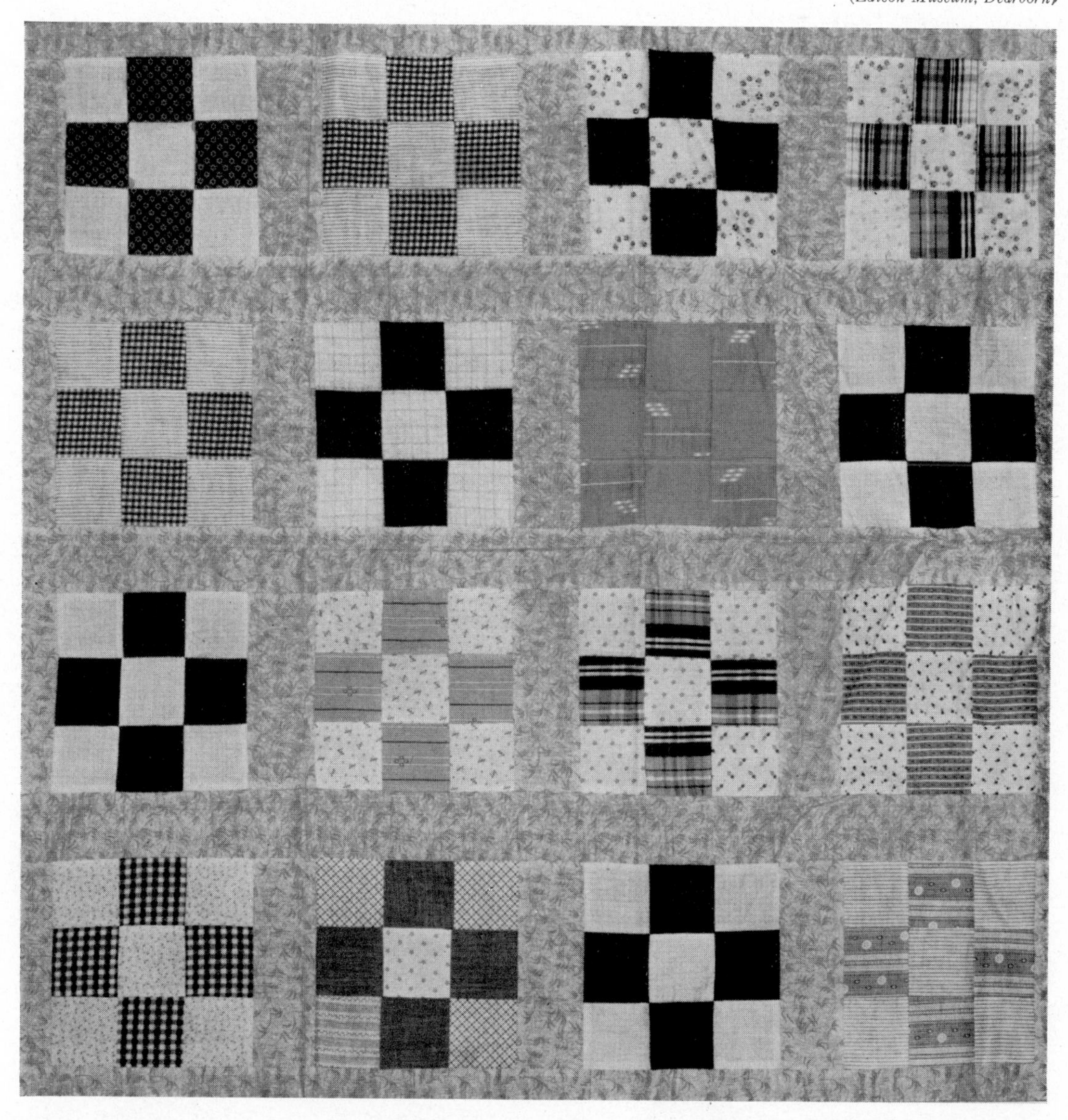

(Courtesy Mrs. Gertrude Smith)

Left: Corner detail of an applique quilt with "Bear's Paw" design. Below: Detail of a quilt with patchwork "Sunburst" in colors on a white ground and appliqued festoons and "Bow Knots" on the border.

(Brooklyn Museum)

(Courtesy, Mrs. Winchell)

Above: Detail of a pieced quilt with "Feathered Star" pattern in shades of pink with white, finely quilted. Below: "Sunburst" and "Feathered Star" pattern in an applique quilt of figured green, plain red and yellow calico. The quilting is in flower vase design. It was made in 1830.

Art Institute of Chicago)

(The Chicago Historical Society)

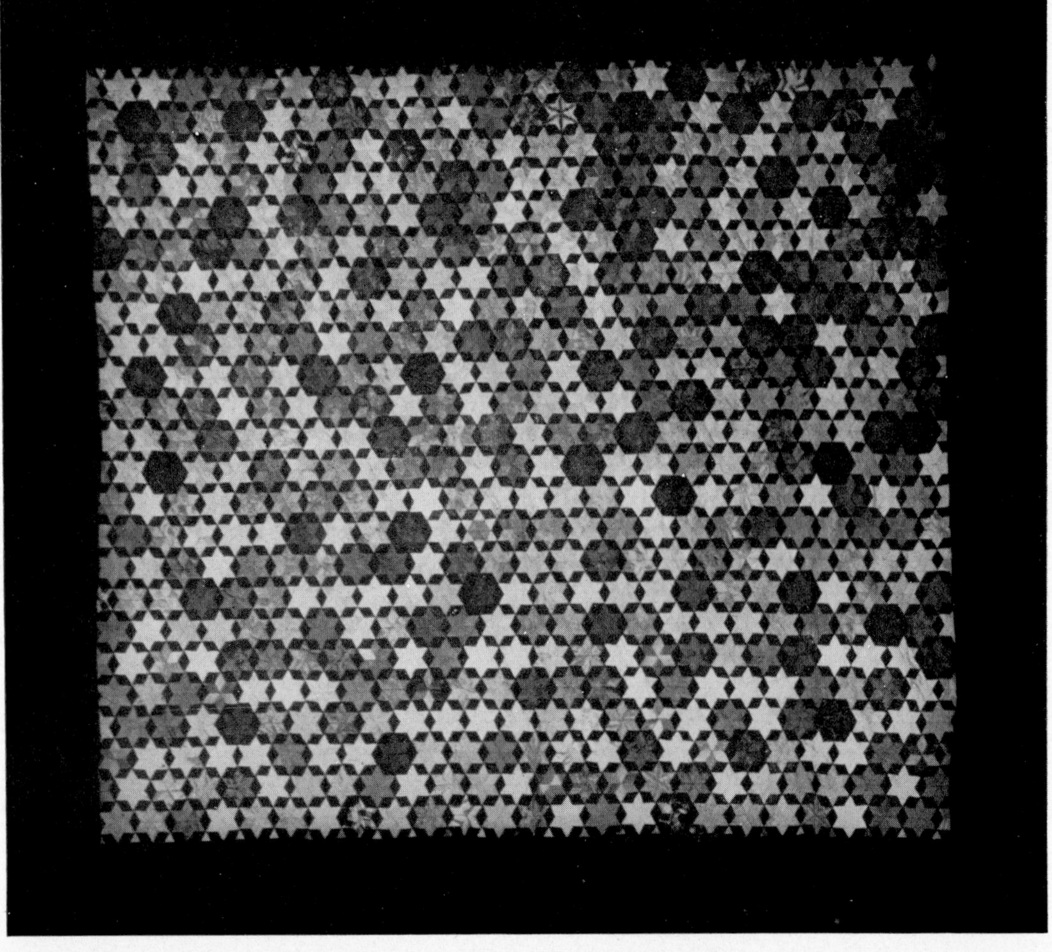

Opposite page, top: A colorful quilt (detail) in mosaic design, made with a variety of colored silks on a plain background. Opposite page, bottom: Quilt of small repeated "Six Pointed Star" design in plain colored materials.

(*Philadelphia Museum of Art*)

(*Art Institute of Chicago*)

bove: "Sunburst" pattern quilt in plain d, green and orange calico with quilting bands of feathers, made in 1850. Top ght: Patchwork quilt of "One Patch," ith exquisite quilting. Right: Detail of "Geometric" block quilt in figured red nd green calico with geometric leaf form uilting.

(*Art Institute of Chicago*)

(*Art Institute of Chicago*)

APPLIQUE QUILTS

(*Art Institute of Chicago*)

Above: Detail of an applique "Circuit Rider" quilt, made in 1862, with 42 squares of various designs in all colors. The quilting in the squares is joined by bands of feather motif. Right: Detail of an applique quilt of "Cherry Tree and Birds" pattern, made in various colored calico about 1820. Opposite page: Pieced "Autograph Quilt" of varied designs appliqued on a plain linen ground, made in 1852 for the Carpenter family, Harrison, New York.

(*Courtesy, Mrs. Leonie G. Tyler*)

(*Brooklyn Museum*)

(*Brooklyn Museum*)

(Prooklyn Museun.)

Above: A beautiful applique quilt designed with red flowers and green leaves in wreaths. Opposite page, top: Detail of a nineteenth century applique quilt with rose pattern in patches of red and green. Opposite page, bottom: Part of an applique quilt with leaf and heart pattern in patches of green and orange. This quilt was also made in the nineteenth century.

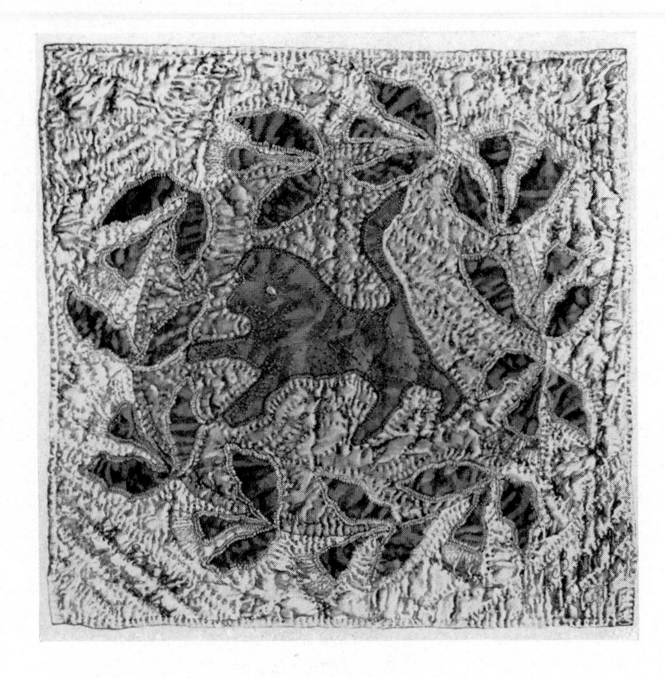

(*Courtesy Daughters of the Utah Pioneers*)

Quilt block of appliqued "Scotch Lion" and thistle emblem, made by Jane S. P. Sharp for a friendship quilt in Salt Lake City. It is made of cotton materials sewn with silk thread.

Opposite page: An ornate applique quilt with exotic embroidered details made by Ann Walgrove Warned. It was begun in 1758 and finished in 1826, in New York.

Part of an appliqued quilt in green, red, orange and yellow on white with diamond pattern in center and garlands of flowers and vines on the sides. It was made in 1840 at Windham, Maine.

(*Courtesy Willis B. Hall*)

(*Metropolitan Museum of Art*)

(*Courtesy, George Reed*)

(*Philadelphia Museum of Art*)

Above: Applique quilt made of cotton prints manufactured by John Hewson, the first printer on cotton in America. The quilt itself was made by Mrs. Hewson, (nee Zibiah Smallwood) in 1800.

Opposite page: Applique quilt made in 1853 of squares of muslin, each with original designs—flower urns, a horse, birds, a little black boy, a dog and a cat, and "things dearest to the maker's heart."

(*Brooklyn Museum*)

Applique quilt made in Baltimore, Maryland, in 1815. Every block has a different design. In many places the material has worn off.

Applique and embroidered quilt, made in 1815 by Mary Rosalie Presstman Myers, Baltimore, Maryland.

(*Brooklyn Museum*)

(*Metropolitan Museum of Art*)

Opposite page: A linen quilt with printed cotton applique, made in Richmond, Virginia, probably by Eliza Armstead Miller to whom it once belonged.

Below: Corner detail of a quilt in floral design, appliqued in calico on muslin. It was made about 1820 in Ohio.

(Courtesy, Mrs. Joseph Baldridge)

(*Art Institute of Chicago*)

Detail of an applique and pieced quilt, made in 1840, with "Princess Feather" pattern and "Cat Track" bands on blocks. Figured green and plain red calico was used, and the quilting is of shell and flower design.

Opposite page: This applique quilt from Damariscotta, Maine, is a variation of the "Orange Peel" design.

Detail of a quilt with "Fern" pattern appliqued in green and scarlet on white cotton. It was made about 1780 in Red Haw, Wayne County, Ohio, by Mary Wellman Eshelman.

(*Courtesy Mrs. Mary Frances Eshelman*)

(Index of American Design)

(*Art Institute of Chicago*)

Detail of an applique quilt with "Forest" pattern in dotted blue calico; the quilting is in diamonds with leaf sprays. It was made in 1861.

(*Courtesy Index of American Design*)

Right: Applique quilt in solid color cottons, made between 1839-1860 in Sonora, Kentucky. Below: "Charter Oak" pattern with other motifs in a detail of an applique quilt made with brown and blue copperplate calico on a plain ground.

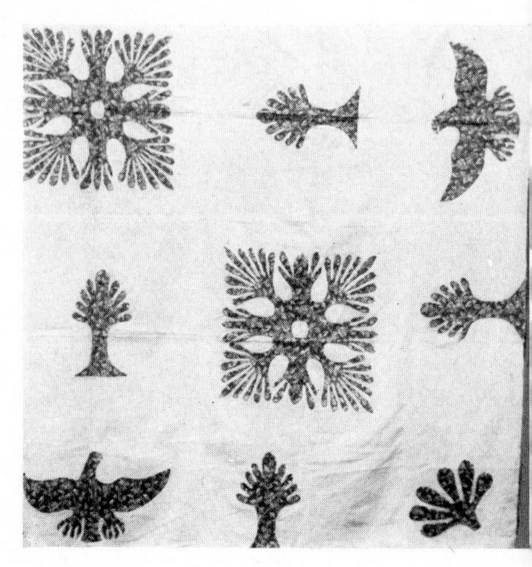

(*Art Institute of Chicago*)

(Courtesy, Mrs. Robert Rue)

Pieced and applique "Album Quilt" in variegated color and fine individual designs, made in 1848 in Hempstead, Long Island, by a "Mrs. Woods."

(Courtesy Mrs. Peggy Westerfield)

Above: Detail of an "Oak Leaf" pattern quilt in green framed squares on white background, appliqued in 1860 in Rockaway Valley, New Jersey. Right: Detail of an applique quilt in "Pomegranite" pattern, made about 1840, with figured green, yellow and pink, plain rose, and red calico. The border is the "Rose Vine" and the quilting is in feather rosettes.

(Art Institute of Chicago)

Opposite page: Unbleached muslin quilt, appliqued in squares with various designs and colors—another example of the "Album Quilt" or "Friendship Quilt." It was made in the middle of the nineteenth century in New Jersey.

Left: The "Tulip" pattern is shown in this detail of an appliqued quilt of red and figured green calico, made between 1845-1850 The quilting is in squares with flowers.

(Art Institute of Chicago)

(*Index of American Design*)

Below center: "Acorn and Oak Leaf" design in quilting made by an early experiment of machine quilting. Below left: The "Ohio Rose" design with a cherry border, made with plain yellow and green and figured red calico on square pattern quilting. This quilt was made about 1845. Below right: Detail of an applique quilt made in 1840, with a "Peony" pattern and tulip border. The material used was figured green and plain red calico with accents of yellow.

Opposite page: An example of the "Martha's Vineyard" pattern in an applique quilt of lavender and green. The fine quilting design is a rosette containing grapes and leaves.

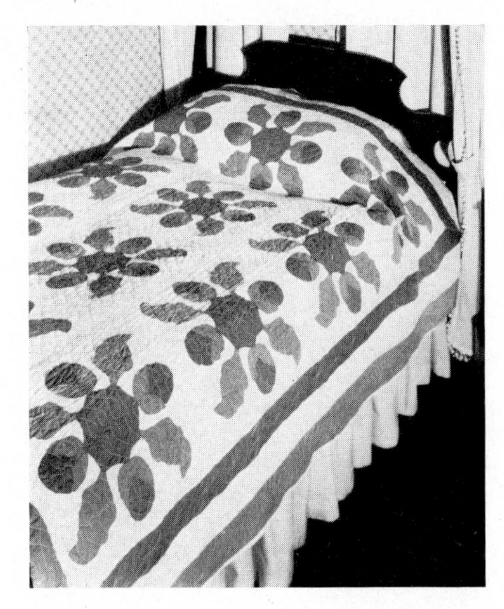

(Courtesy, Stearns & Foster Co.)

(Art Institute of Chicago)

(Art Institute of Chicago)

(Courtesy, Stearns & Foster Co.)

(*Art Institute of Chicago*)

(*Art Institute of Chicago*)

Above: An example of the "Whig Rose" pattern in figured green and pink, plain red and yellow calico. Right: The "Rose Wreath" pattern, in red and green calico with quilting in checks and a vine border. Lower right: An example of the "Pumpkin Blossom" pattern, in plain red, green and yellow calico. The irregular quilting was done on the first Howe sewing machine, brought into Michigan between 1845-1850. The examples on this and the opposite page are details.

(*Art Institute of Chicago*)

(*Art Institute of Chicago*)

Left: The "Heart and Dart" pattern in an applique quilt with turkey red calico and diagonal design quilting. Below Left: An example of the "Pineapple" pattern on an applique quilt made around 1852. Plain green and red calico was used and the quilting is in a garden flower design. Below: The "Poinsettia" pattern in a quilt made in 1850, with figured blue and green and plain red calico. The quilting is in squares.

(*Art Institute of Chicago*)

(*Art Institute of Chicago*)

(Art Institute of Chicago)

Above: Detail of a quilt showing the "Oriental Poppy" pattern, made with figured green and pink and plain red calico. The quilting is in small squares. Right: Detail of an appliqued quilt in squares with varied floral and star designs.

(Index of American Design)

(Courtesy, Mrs. Frederick Piester)

"Inlay Eagle," a formal white cotton applique quilt with colored chintz and calico, made about 1820 in West Virginia.

(Courtesy, Mr. Roger Benjamin

Above: Small detail of an appliqued quilt on muslin, made 1840-1860 somewhere between Baltimore and Philadelphia
Below: Detail of a quilt with applique and embroidery, made in the nineteenth century at York, Pennsylvania. The white cotton top is unquilted, the applique is in plain colored and one figure cotton, fastened down with a variety of embroidery stitches The edges are buttonholed.

(Courtesy, Mrs. Bentley Stevenson)

(*Courtesy, Mrs. John D. Rockefeller, Jr.*)

Applique quilt made in the middle of the nineteenth century in Pennsylvania. It has 25 applique blocks in the style of painted velvet. Two blocks show the eagle holding the Flag, one block bears the word "Texas," and one "Lone Red Star" which leads authorities to believe this quilt celebrated the independence of Texas, or its admission to the Union in 1845.

ALL-WHITE QUILT

(*Art Institute of Chicago*)

(*Courtesy, Mrs. Gertrude Smith*)

Above: An example of the contemporary American quilt, designed and executed by Mrs. Gertrude Smith. It is named "E Pluribus Unum." On the sides of the center design of this red quilt are the seals of the four states from which her ancestors came. The design is stuffed and the background is in diamond quilting. It is interesting to compare this example to the one on the opposite page, made in 1822. This "All White" quilt (of which this is a corner detail) has an elaborate pattern with double border, and a vase of flowers in the center. Examples such as these rely entirely upon the skill in quilting for their effect.

(*Mrs. B. Stenge*)

Another modern quilt, made on a cream background. The "Lotus Flowers" are in three shades of pink, the leaves are green and the border is green with small red circles. The quilting is in small feathered wreaths and squares. It was made by Mrs. B. Stenge.

The illustrations above and on the next page are of quilts made by the author. Above is an applique quilt with repeated floral design and border on a white quilted background.

A garland of flowers in pink, dark rose and light blue, on a white background. The scrolls are a middle green and the leaves dark green. This modern quilt was designed and made by the author.

SOURCES OF DESIGN

The examples on this and ensuing pages show the type of source from which many quilt makers obtained ideas for their own designs. Below: Stuffed and quilted bureau cover, made between 1821-1825, with basket of fruit design and leaf vine border.

(*Metropolitan Museum of Art*)

(*Metropolitan Museum of Art*)

Details taken from a 1770 crewel embroidered bedspread, designed and made by Mary Breed in Boston. The birds, trees, berries, and leaves are embroidered in Oriental stitch in wool on linen, the trefoils are embroidered in chevron stitch, while buttonhole stitch outlines the leaves and birds. Opposite page: Linen bedspread (eighteenth century) with colored crewel embroidery. Examples of crewel embroidery like this were seen by the quiltmakers and may likely have also been made by many of these same craftsmen.

(Brooklyn Museum)

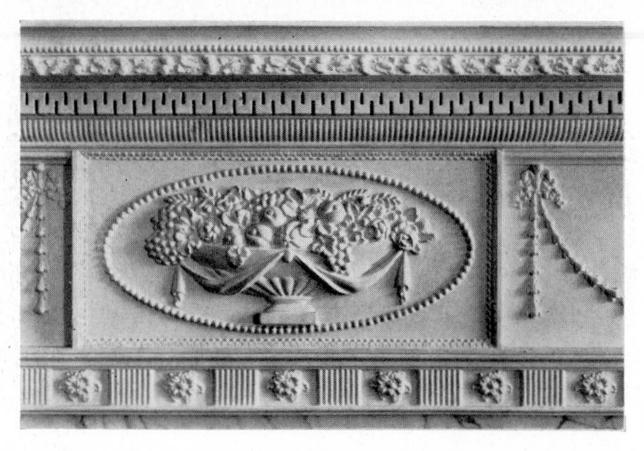

Elaborate wood carving, such as these two examples, suggested designs for quilts and embroidery. The one at the left is on a mantel in Pingree House, the one on the right is in the Pierce-Nichols House, both in Salem, Massachusetts.

(*Photos: courtesy Samuel Chamberlain*)

Below: This late eighteenth century American coverlet, probably made by the Pennsylvania Dutch, could also have suggested a motif for many a quilt design.

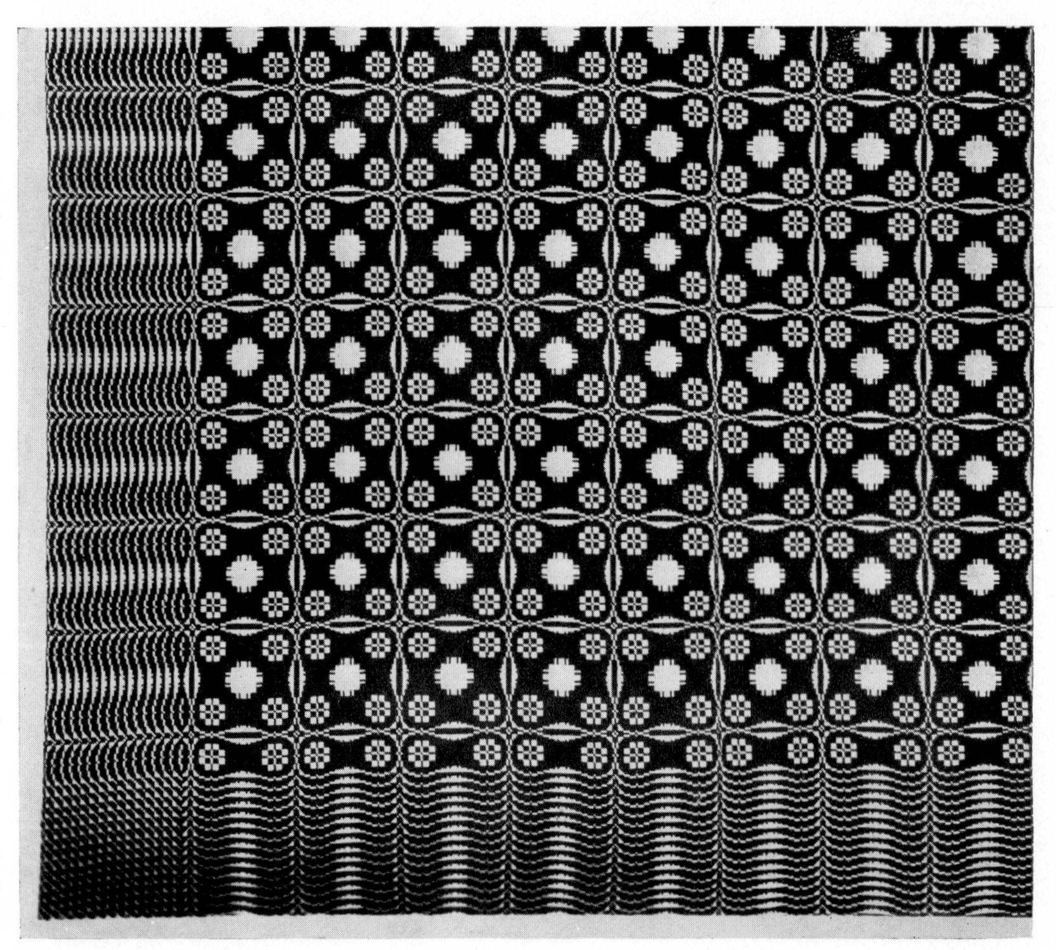

(*Brooklyn Museum*)

(*Photo; courtesy, Samuel Chamberlain*)

Above: A further example of wood carving, also a plate and tiles. The pottery and chinaware of the time provided another source of design for the quiltmakers. This illustration is from a room in the Wentworth-Gardner House, Portsmouth.

Right: This coverlet which was the work of an itinerent weaver, contains stars, rosettes and eagles—typical motifs used in embroidery and quilts.

(*Art Institute of Chicago*)

(1)

(Art Institute of Chicago)

(The Chicago Historical Society) (2

(3)

(Courtesy Index of American Design)

(4)

(5) (*Art Institute of Chicago*)

(*The Chicago Historical Society*) (6)

Other design sources are illustrated on this and the opposite page: (1) The front panel and the side panels of Johnson's tailor's stove might have been adapted to quilt designs. (2) "Large Squaw" shows the Victorian influence—button shoes, light waist, hour glass figure. Note also, Court presentation plumes. (3) A wedding chest of painted wood. The front view of the rose and the profile view of the tulip are characteristics of Pennsylvania Dutch artists. The stars also suggest the many star quilt blocks. (4) The Conestoga Wagon. (5) The blue Staffordshire plate with the "Bill of Rights." The eagles in the border and the scrolls were often used on quilts. (6) Ship's figurehead from schooner engaged in Great Lakes trading. Mary Gregory, 1875. The embellishments suggest designs for a quilt border. (These examples are only a few of the many types of influences that inspired quilt makers.)

This fine bedspread, embroidered in colored worsted, was made in the nineteenth century.

BIBLIOGRAPHY

ABBOT, EDITH — "Women in Industry; a Study in American Economic History." D. Appleton & Co., New York, 1910.

ADAMS, JAMES TRUSLOW — "The Epic of America." 1931. "New England in the Republic." 1926. Little, Brown and Company.

BAGNALL, WILLIAM RHODES — "The Textile Industries of the United States," Vol. 1. (1639-1810.) Riverside Press, Cambridge, Mass., 1893. "Samuel Slater and The Early Development of the Cotton Manufacture in the United States." J. S. Stewart, Middleton, Connecticut, 1890.

BAKER, GEORGE PERCIVAL — "Calico Painting and Printing in the East Indies in the XVII and XVIII Centuries." London, 1921.

BARBER, EDWIN ATLEE — "Tulip Ware of the Pennsylvania-German Potters." Philadelphia, Patterson & White. 1903.

BISHOP, JOHN LEANDER — "History of American Manufactures, from 1608-1860." E. Young, Philadelphia, 1861.

CAMEHL, ADA WALKER — "The Blue China Book." E. P. Dutton, 1916.

CANDEE, HELEN CHURCHILL — "Weaves and Draperies." Frederick Stokes Co. 1930.

CAPEY, RECO — "The Printing of Textiles." Chapman & Hall, 1930.

CARRICK, ALICE VAN LEER — "Collector's Luck." "Early American Hooked Rugs." Atlantic Monthly Press. 1919.

CHAMBERLAIN, SAMUEL — "Beyond New England Thresholds." Hastings House, New York, 1937.

CLARK, VICTOR SELDEN — "History of Manufactures in the United States, 1607-1860." Carnegie Institute, Washington, 1916.

CLOUZOT, HENRI — "Painted and Printed Fabrics." Metropolitan Museum.

COPELAND, MELVIN THOMAS — "The Cotton Manufacturing Industry of the United States." Harvard University, Cambridge, 1912.

CRAWFORD, MORRIS DE CAMP — "The Heritage of Cotton." G. P. Putnam's Sons, 1924.

CROUSE, RUSSEL — "Mr. Currier and Mr. Ives." Doubleday Doran, 1930.

EARLE, ALICE MORSE — "Costume of Colonial Times." Charles Scribner Sons, New York, 1917. "Home Life in Colonial Days." 1898. "Child Life in Colonial Days." 1899. MacMillan, New York.

EATON, ALLEN HENDERSHOTT — "Handicrafts of the Southern Highlands." Russell Sage Foundation, New York, 1937.

EBERLEIN, MCCLURE & HOLLOWAY — "The Practical Book of Interior Decoration." J. B. Lippincott Co., 1919.

EBERLEIN, DONALDSON, MCCLURE — "The Practical Book of American Antiques." Garden City Publishing Co., New York, 1936.

FINLEY, RUTH E. — "Old Patchwork Quilts and the Women Who Made Them." J. B. Lippincott Co., 1929.

FIELD, EDWARD — "State of Rhode Island and Providence Plantations at the End of the Century." Mason Co., Boston, 1902.

HALL, ELIZA CALVERT — "Aunt Jane of Kentucky." (1907.) "Book of Hand-Woven Coverlets." 1912. Little, Brown & Co.

HALL, CARRIE A., AND KRETSINGER, ROSE GOOD — "The Romance of the Patchwork Quilt in America." The Caxton Printers, 1936.

HARBESON, GEORGIANA BROWN — "American Needlework." Coward-McCann, 1938.

HAWTHORNE, NATHANIEL — "The Marble Faun." Houghton, Mifflin & Co., 1899.

Howells, John Mead — "Architectural Heritage of the Piscataqua." Architectural Book Publishing Co., New York, 1937.

Jourdain, Margaret — "Regency Furniture." Country Life, London. 1934.

Kauffman, Henry — "Pennsylvania Dutch-American Folk Art." Studio Publications, Inc., New York, 1946.

Kettell, Russell Hawes — "Pine Furniture of Early New England." Doubleday, Doran & Co., New York, 1929.

Kent, William Winthrop — "The Hooked Rug." Dodd, Mead & Co., 1931.

King, Elizabeth — "Quilting." Leisure League of America. 1934.

Lamb, J. H. — "Lamb's Textile Industries in the United States." J. H. Lamb, Boston, 1916. (2 vols.)

Little, Frances — "Early American Textiles." Century Co., 1931.

Larcom, Lucy — "A New England Girlhood Outlined from Memory." Houghton, Mifflin, 1890.

Lee, Ruth Webb — "Early American Pressed Glass." Northboro, Mass., 1931.

Lockwood, Sarah McNeil — "Antiques." Doubleday, 1925.

Lockwood, Luke Vincent — "Colonial Furniture in America." (1926.) "Early American Wall Paintings." (1931.) Charles Scribner Sons.

Lodge, Henry Cabot — "Early Memories." Charles Scribner Sons, 1913.

Matschat, Cecile — "Suwannee River." Farrar and Rinehart, N. Y., 1938.

McClelland, Nancy — "Furnishing the Colonial and Federal House." Lippincott, 1936. "Duncan Phyfe and the English Regency." W. R. Scott, New York, 1939.

McKim, Ruby Short — "One Hundred and One Patchwork Patterns." McKim Studios, Independence, Mo., 1931.

Morse, Frances Clary — "Furniture of the Olden Time." Macmillan, 1902.

Northend, Mary Harrod — "American Glass." Dodd, Mead & Co., 1926.

Nutting, Wallace — "Furniture of the Pilgrim Century." Old America Company, 1924.

O'Neil, Charles — A Dictionary of Calico Printing and Dyeing. Simpkin, Marshall & Co. London, 1862.

Osburn, Burl N. — "Measured Drawings of Early American Furniture." Bruce Publishing Co., Milwaukee, 1926.

Percival, MacIver — "The Chintz Book." Frederick Stokes, New York, 1923.

Pitkin, Albert Hastings — "Early American Folk Pottery." Case, Lockwood and Brainard, Hartford, Conn. 1918.

Pepperell Mfg. Co. — "The Romance of Pepperell." Biddeford, Maine.

Rice, Alice Caldwell Hegan — "Mrs. Wiggs of The Cabbage Patch." Century Co.

Singleton, Esther — "The Furniture of Our Forefathers." Doubleday, 1913.

Small, Cassie Paine — "How to Know Textiles." Ginn, Boston, 1932.

Spargo, John — "Early American Pottery and China." The Century Co., New York and London, 1926.

Tassin, Algernon — "The Magazine in America." Dodd, Mead & Co., 1916.

Victoria and Albert Museum — "A Brief Guide to the Oriental Painted, Dyed and Printed Textiles." "A Brief Guide to the Western Painted, Dyed and Printed Textiles." London, 1924.

Walton, Perry — "The Story of Textiles." Walton Co., 1925.

Waring, Janet — "Early American Stencils on Walls and Furniture." W. R. Scott, New York, 1937.

Webster, Marie D. — "Quilts: Their Story and How to Make Them." Doubleday, Doran & Co., 1928.